IMAGES
of America

CENTRAL FLORIDA'S CIVIL WAR VETERANS

This map, published by J.H. Colton of New York, depicts Central Florida as it appeared shortly before Polk County was established on February 8, 1861. On January 10, 1861, a month prior to the county's establishment, Florida had voted to secede from the Union. In April, two short months after Polk entered as Florida's newest county, the War Between the States erupted in Charleston Harbor, South Carolina. (Author's collection.)

On the Cover: In 1920, the United Daughters of the Confederacy held a Confederate veterans' reunion picnic at the home of Thomas and Fannie Hall to celebrate Robert E. Lee's birthday. The Hall house in Leesburg, Lake County, was called Three Oaks. Confederate veteran Thomas Kennedy Hall is seated in the second row at far right. Members of the Children of the Confederacy are seated on the ground with one of Leesburg's trademark watermelons. (Courtesy of the Leesburg Heritage Society.)

IMAGES
of America

CENTRAL FLORIDA'S CIVIL WAR VETERANS

Bob Grenier

ARCADIA
PUBLISHING

ISBN 978-1-4671-1202-4

Published by Arcadia Publishing
Charleston, South Carolina

Printed in the United States of America

Library of Congress Control Number: 2013955322

For all general information, please contact Arcadia Publishing:
Telephone 843-853-2070
Fax 843-853-0044
E-mail sales@arcadiapublishing.com
For customer service and orders:
Toll-Free 1-888-313-2665

Visit us on the Internet at www.arcadiapublishing.com

Dedicated to my family and friends, who inspire me to treasure and preserve our history, as well as to the memory of all the veterans and their families—North and South!

Contents

ACKNOWLEDGMENTS

I am very grateful to everyone who made this photographic journey through Central Florida history possible, including Lois Murphy, Carolyn McGraw, Sheila Tindle, Kay McGee, Lloyd Harris, Delicia Wallnofer, Maria Trippe, Patricia Weeks, Nelson Winbush, Vince Bronson, Jean Witherington, Kristy Mcary, Liz Stemm, Terry Torrens, Kimber Davis, Bob Lovell, Don Campbell, Sandy Mott, Jerry Peacock, Judy Rainey, Chief Carle Bishop, Howard King, Don Polly, Victor Smith III, Andrea Binkley, Gidget Gibson, Mary Jo and Mal Martin, Jeff Grzelak, Shirley Cannon, Larry Leudenburg, Ron Alcorn, Lisa Stanley, Tom Roberts, Fred Donaldson, Billy DeSilva, Gloria Williams, Tom Wilcox, Ann Williams, John Thrasher, Sheri White, Susan Buckley, Darlene Walker, Mel and Gary Haynes, Catherine and Byron Peavy, Karen and Harry Hurst, Judy and Jim Davis, and my nephew Andrew Peterson. I would also like to thank Prof. Wenxian Zhang, Darla Moore, and Angelina Altobellis of Rollins College; author Jim Robison for sharing his historical research and his extensive collection of photographs; Alma Grenier for her research, photography, and being the model for Lola Sánchez; and the Tavares Public Library reference librarian, Marli Wilkins, for her research, editing, and proofreading.

There are many outstanding organizations to thank, including the United Daughters of the Confederacy, Sons of Confederate Veterans, Order of Confederate Rose, Leesburg Masonic Lodge, Polk County History Center, St. Cloud Heritage Museum, Osceola Historical Society, Greater Dunnellon Historical Society, Micanopy Historical Society Archives, Apopka Historical Society, Maitland Historical Society, West Volusia Historical Society, Geneva Historical Society, Oviedo Historical Society, Seminole County Historical Society, Sanford Museum, Sanford Student Museum, Central Florida Society for Historic Preservation, Leesburg Heritage Society, Wildwood Historical Association, Lake County Historical Society, Alachua County Library, Putnam County Library, Haines City Public Library, Lakeland Public Library, the Library of Congress, the Virginia Military Institute, and the State Archives of Florida, which was an invaluable resource.

I wish to thank my friends at Arcadia Publishing: Joe Walker, Maggie Bullwinkel, Liz Gurley, and Jennifer Sexton.

This book was made possible by the support and encouragement of my Mom and Dad, Wahine, Flash, Capt. Melton Haynes, and, of course, God!

Introduction

While the War Between the States was raging through the Shenandoah Valley, along the Rappahannock River, up and down the Mississippi Valley, high in the Tennessee Mountains, along the Missouri-Kansas border, and in a small rural town in southern Pennsylvania, south of the Georgia border, the Blue and the Gray were engaged in a struggle to control the scrub and brush, the sand and swamps, and the pines and palmettos of the warm, feral Florida frontier.

Celebrated national figures, such as Robert E. Lee, George Meade, Thomas "Stonewall" Jackson, Philip Sheridan, Nathan Bedford Forrest, William T. Sherman, J.E.B. Stuart, and Ulysses S. Grant were garnering headlines as they tangled at center stage. Meanwhile, more obscure men such as J.J. Dickison, Albert Wilcoxson, Winston Stephens, William Birney, Charles Munnerlyn, Melton Haynes, William Noble, and George Washington Bronson gave their last full measure without national fanfare.

With the bombardment and surrender of Fort Sumter at Charleston Harbor in April 1861, the War Between the States commenced. Believing the war would be short-lived when the diversely clad armies of the North and South battled at First Manassas on July 21, 1861, Florida combatants traveled north to join neighboring states' regiments. But soon, the need of Florida's resources became vital. Cattle, salt, sugar, turpentine, cotton, citrus, and other crops were in demand. Also, the Florida peninsula, with its endless miles of coastline, provided strategic military positions, as well as hundreds of ports and harbors from which to launch trade routes to Europe, the Caribbean, and the Gulf states. By 1862, the intriguing tale of Florida's venture into America's bloodiest conflict began.

There are many great books and publications about the military strategies, political ambitions, and skirmishes and battles that took place in Florida during the War Between the States, but *Central Florida's Civil War Veterans* provides a personal look into the lives of the men and women, from both sides of the Mason-Dixon Line, who entered the annals of Florida's history. The images contained within these pages will give the reader an in-depth look into the faces of those who shaped the "Eastern Frontier." *Central Florida's Civil War Veterans* serves as a memorial and tribute to those courageous veterans and their families who endured through this tumultuous time in American history.

Following Robert E. Lee's surrender at Appomattox Court House in April 1865, an aftermath of destruction lay over the countryside. In addition to the ravaged land, there was the tremendous loss of American lives. Separated families, shattered dreams, lost livelihoods, fatal illnesses, broken hearts, and scores of cemeteries appeared as the smoke settled on the battlefields. A wilderness, deep in the heart of Florida, remained relatively unscathed. Soon, families from Pennsylvania and New York, Virginia and the Carolinas, Illinois and Ohio, and Tennessee and Alabama, packed what remained of their lives and traveled to Florida to begin a new life.

A month following Lee's surrender, Florida's brave "Knight," Capt. J.J. Dickison, addressed the loyal defenders of Florida:

> Brother Officers and Soldiers: The time has arrived when, with sorrow, your commanding officer must bid you farewell. Many of you have, for nearly three years, been my pride and admiration. Your noble deeds of heroism have crowned you with glory and renown, and whatever honor I have won, you have proudly shared it with me. To separate myself from such men, after the relationship, which has existed between us, is a severe trial. Although many reverses have attended us during the past thirty days, I am proud to know we are not whipped—only overpowered. We stand firm, unshaken, united. Want of ammunition and provisions compelled our noble armies to succumb—deeply do we sympathize with them. In separating from you, my brave companions, I feel as if the nearest ties of brotherhood were to be severed forever. Farewell, my brave soldiers; return to your homes, and take with you the assurance that, whatever may be my destiny; I shall ever look to this command with gratitude and pride. Farewell! Affectionately farewell!

The following pages of vintage photographs showcase just a fragment of the fascinating people and time-altering events that shaped each of these Central Florida communities. Each county featured in *Central Florida's Civil War Veterans* spotlights those men and women, whether Union or Confederate, aristocracy or commoner, magnates or working-class citizens, who made a lasting impression in their region.

The final chapter takes the reader beyond the borders of Central Florida, to every corner of the peninsula. Readers will cross Paynes Prairie with the "Cow Cavalry," cruise the St. Johns River on the USS *Columbine*, cross Natural Bridge to Tallahassee, battle blockade runners on Tampa Bay, sail to Fort Jefferson in the Dry Tortugas, and set up camp at Olustee. Also featured in this exciting bonus chapter are a few of the many dedicated people who preserve, teach, and honor the memory of the region's Civil War veterans and who hope to inspire future generations to continue their work.

People from all over the world travel to Central Florida to experience the thrilling theme parks and attractions, where they can dance and sing with cartoon characters, save the world with costumed superheroes, ride upside-down on corkscrew roller coasters, and get splashed by performing whales. Central Florida offers much more! The area is home to many county and municipal historical societies, museums, state parks, heritage trails, and historic sites. The author encourages residents and tourists to visit these places to learn more about the men and women who settled their communities, and their roles in the War Between the States.

One

Imperial Polk County
The Heart of Florida

In 1861, Polk County was established as Florida's 39th county, named for the 11th president of the United States, James Knox Polk. Confederate and Union veterans who settled in Polk built the county into one of Florida's most prominent cattle, phosphate, and agricultural centers. Shown here is the marble statue of a Southern soldier atop the Confederate monument in Munn Park in Lakeland. (Courtesy of Alma Nevarez Grenier.)

Francis Stebbins Bartow, a Georgia attorney and political figure, was born in Savannah in 1816. Bartow served as a Confederate colonel and died on July 21, 1861, from wounds he received leading a charge at the Battle of First Manassas. In 1862, Polk County changed the name of its county seat from Fort Blount to Bartow to honor the Confederate war hero. (Courtesy of the Polk County History Center.)

Col. Henry Stephen Haines was a successful railroad developer and engineer who was instrumental in the success of Henry Plant's railroad system. Haines was born in Nantucket, Massachusetts, in 1836. During the War Between the States, he was in charge of maintaining military transportation service in the Carolinas. In 1887, the Polk County town of Clay Cut changed its name to Haines City. (Courtesy of the Haines City Public Library.)

Prior to receiving the iconic "Stonewall" moniker at the Battle of First Manassas, West Point graduate Thomas Jackson served as first lieutenant of Company E, 1st US Artillery at Fort Meade from December 1850 to May 1851. His primary duty was to scout for renegade Seminoles. In 1851, Jackson resigned his commission to become a professor at the Virginia Military Academy in Lexington. (Courtesy of the Virginia Military Academy.)

Erected by the Polk County Historical Commission, this marker indicates the location of Fort Meade. From 1849 to 1858, the fort served as a military headquarters during the Seminole Indian Wars. It was built by, and named for, Lt. George Gordon Meade, who in 1863 became the Union commander at Gettysburg. As an engineer, Meade designed Florida's Jupiter Inlet Light and Sombrero Key Light. (Courtesy of Alma Nevarez Grenier.)

In this 1889 photograph of the Florida Senate, John Wesley Bryant is in the first row, third from right. He arrived in Polk County in 1856 at the age of 12. Bryant enlisted in the Confederate States Army, serving in several companies, including Col. Charles Munnerlyn's Florida Cow Cavalry. Bryant was a powerful political and financial leader in Polk County, where he resided for 68 years. He died in 1926. (Courtesy of State Archives of Florida.)

Physician James Appleton Chapman was born on March, 13, 1835, in Macon County, Alabama. Chapman received his medical degree in 1859 and returned to Alabama to set up his practice. In 1861, he mustered into the 4th Alabama Regiment, Company B. In 1882, he and his wife, Elizabeth, moved to Polk County. Here, Dr. Chapman relaxes at his home in Kathleen around 1910. (Courtesy of Barbara Buckley Kerschner.)

Gen. Evander McIver Law was the commander of the Alabama Brigade, also known as "Laws' Brigade." Law moved to Florida in 1881, and in 1895, he established the South Florida Military Institute in Bartow. As a trustee of the Summerlin Institute and a member of the Polk County Board of Education, Law was a major influence in Florida's public education system. (Courtesy of the Polk County History Center.)

In 1863, Confederate hero James Abner Cox was wounded in the siege of Vicksburg and was held as a prisoner of war in Ohio at Johnson's Island in Sandusky Bay. In 1889, he and his wife, Mary, moved to Polk County, where he served in the Florida legislature. Cox died in 1923 and is buried in Lakeland. The inscription on his gravestone reads, "He Fought a Good Fight." (Courtesy of Hampton Dunn.)

Elias Holman Tyler was born in 1825 in South Carolina. In 1858, he married Obedience Carter. In 1860, soon after the birth of their son James, they moved to Lowndes County, Georgia. In September 1861, Tyler enlisted in the 26th Georgia Infantry. After he was medically discharged in 1862, they moved to Florida, eventually settling in Fort Meade in 1880. Tyler died there in 1915. (Courtesy of Delicia Maguire Wallnofer.)

Edward Gross Wilder and his wife, Cornelia, lived in Socrum. He served as fourth sergeant in Capt. John T. Lesley's Company B, Florida Cavalry. In a note to *Confederate Veteran* magazine, Wilder wrote, "I surrendered my musket to the Federal officer at Fort Brook, Tampa, Fla. in May, 1865. Since then I have marched side by side in parade with the gray and the blue." (Courtesy of Lois Sherrouse Murphy.)

Claytus Sherouse was born in 1826. In July 1843, he applied for a land patent in Marion County, Florida. He traveled to Irwin County, Georgia, in 1848 and married Mary Grantham. Sherouse enlisted in Company F, 9th Florida Infantry in February 1863 in Marion County. He was slightly wounded at the Battle of Olustee in 1864. By 1870, Sherouse moved his family to Polk County. (Courtesy of Lois Sherrouse Murphy.)

In 1859, John William and Sarah Ann Harris Costine traveled by wagon from South Carolina to Florida and settled in an area known as Foxtown, west of Polk City. John Costine enlisted in the Florida Cavalry in Hillsborough County, serving under Capt. John T. Lesley in Munnerlyn's Brigade. Following the war, Costine became a successful cattle rancher. He died in 1922 in Auburndale. (Painting by Renata Pastula, courtesy of Lois Sherrouse Murphy.)

Enoch Everett Mizell was born on June 18, 1841, in North Florida. He married Martha Ann Bryant in Polk County on January 20, 1864. In April 1862, Mizell enlisted in Company B, 7th Florida Infantry. He was appointed to the board of county commissioners in Polk County in 1865. Mizell also served Polk as sheriff, tax collector, assessor, and in the Florida House of Representatives. (Courtesy of Lois Sherrouse Murphy.)

Augustus Columbus Thompson was born on January 16, 1828, in Jackson County, Georgia. He married Mary Arline Randolph on December 1, 1850. In 1861, Thompson enlisted as a captain in Company G, 16th Georgia Infantry. In 1880, the Thompsons moved to Lakeland, where, in 1882, Thompson contracted with the Polk County Commission to take charge of the county's first "poor farm." Thompson died in 1905. (Courtesy of Sheila McMullen Tindle.)

Born in 1823 in North Carolina, Streaty Parker was eight when his family moved to Columbia County, Florida, where, in 1848, he married Mary Eve Blount. The couple traveled with Mary's family to what is now Polk County in 1851. In 1861, Parker was elected captain of a Confederate militia unit called the "Hickory Boys." Later, he joined Munnerlyn's 1st Florida Special Cavalry. Parker died in 1884. (Courtesy of State Archives of Florida.)

David McMullen was born in 1835 in Georgia. In 1861, he enlisted in Company I, 2nd Florida Cavalry CSA. The unit fought at Olustee, Gainesville, and Braddock's Farm, and was paroled at Waldo in May 1865. In 1866, McMullen married Keturah Loretta Campbell. They had seven children. In 1886, McMullen married Lucy Youmans (pictured) in Lakeland, where they operated the Sunshine Hotel. McMullen died in 1896. (Courtesy of Sheila McMullen Tindle.)

John Perry Reynolds (seated, center) was born in 1845 in Georgia. In 1863, Reynolds enlisted in the 1st Regiment Infantry Reserves CSA near Fort Meade. He was never formally discharged. He was in Fort Meade when he learned that the war was over. Reynolds married Sarah Ann Barton on February 13, 1870, in Orlando. In 1883, he began farming pine timber. Reynolds died in 1918. (Courtesy of Sheila McMullen Tindle.)

Annie Hanna Darracott was born in Alabama in 1861. Her father served in the 4th Alabama Infantry. Annie married Thomas Jefferson Darracott in 1882. The couple moved to Lakeland in 1895. Annie founded the Lakeland chapter of the United Daughters of the Confederacy (UDC) in 1904 and spearheaded the effort to erect the Confederate monument in Munn Park in 1910. Annie died in 1956 and is buried in Lakeland. (Courtesy of Carolyn Warner McGraw.)

In October 1910, Bartow hosted the 20th annual United Confederate Veterans Convention and Reunion. The previous year, it had been held in Live Oak in Suwannee County. The Classical Revival architecture of the newly constructed Polk County courthouse provided the backdrop for these photographs. The courthouse, Polk County's third, was located at the corner of Main Street and Broadway Avenue. It was built by the Mutual Construction Company of Louisville, Kentucky, and was designed by architect Edward Columbus Hosford. It was completed in 1909, in time for this milestone reunion. Clement Anselm Evans, one of the founders of the United Confederate Veterans (UCV) in 1889, was the commander in chief of the organization at the time of this reunion. In the above photograph, note that all of the veterans are wearing their 20th-anniversary reunion ribbon and medallion. (Both, courtesy of the Polk County History Center.)

During the first week of November 1914, the UCV mustered in Lakeland. The "Welcome" arch, which spanned Kentucky Avenue, greeted the veterans. Nathan Bedford Forrest II, grandson of Confederate general Nathan Bedford Forrest, was one of the reunion's notable attendees. Forrest II was the adjutant in chief of the Sons of Confederate Veterans. The *Tampa Tribune* reported, "General Forrest expressed himself as highly pleased with Lakeland, and as being hopeful that he can return later with his wife and family to spend a portion of the winter here." The reunion festivities included Annie Darracott hosting a reception for the maids and sponsors, and veterans reminiscing by a campfire in Munn Park. Below, Mabel Drane drives a Rambler, with Herbert McMullen seated beside her. (Above, artwork by Andrew Peterson; bottom, courtesy of the Polk County History Center.)

The Lakeland chapter of the UDC dedicated this Confederate monument on June 3, 1910. It is located in Munn Park, which was named for city founder Abraham Munn. Attorney general and future governor Park Trammell was the dedication's keynote speaker. The monument, which stands 26 feet tall, was manufactured by the McNeel Marble Company of Marietta, Georgia. It features an east-facing Confederate soldier standing at parade rest, hands on his Enfield rifle. The photograph at right features the Lakeland UDC in 1915. Annie Darracott is standing in the second row, sixth from the left. Below, UDC members from the Annie H. Darracott 791, Plant City 1931, and William Anderson Sanders 2474 chapters gather on May 15, 2010, to rededicate the monument on its 100th anniversary. (Right, courtesy of State Archives of Florida; below, courtesy of Carolyn Warner McGraw.)

Musician Maude Howe Johnson Chenette (at left in the photograph at left) was a "real" daughter of the Confederacy. She composed and published the song "Daughters of the UDC" in 1970 in Orlando. Chenette was 95 when she attended this monument unveiling on July 3, 1982, in Bartow. She was the daughter of William Hampton Johnson, first sergeant of Company E, 7th Florida Infantry Regiment, known as the "South Florida Bulldogs," whom the monument honors. The monument was erected by the Gen. Evander McIver Law Camp No. 1323 of Lakeland. The inscription on the monument reads, "In memory of the 79 militia men under command of Capt. Nathan S. Blount who marched from this site to Gainesville to muster into the CS Army rendering gallant service from April 10, 1862–April 26, 1865." (Both, courtesy of the Polk County History Center.)

Two

Osceola County Cracker Cowboys and the GAR

Osceola County, named for the celebrated Seminole warrior Osceola, was established on May 12, 1887. The city of Kissimmee, originally called Allendale, after Confederate major J.H. Allen, was incorporated in 1883. The city of St. Cloud was established in 1909 as a retirement community for Union veterans. Shown here is a Grand Army of the Republic reunion in Kissimmee on May 20, 1912. (Courtesy of the Osceola County Historical Society.)

George Washington Bronson enlisted in 1861 in the 1st Florida Infantry Battalion. He served in Florida from the east coast to the Apalachicola River. After the Battle of Olustee, Bronson came down with typhoid fever and was hospitalized in Lake City. In 1865, his unit was assigned to guard the Suwannee River at Clay's Landing. He married Margaret Ann Goodman in 1867. Bronson died in 1910. (Courtesy of Vince Bronson.)

William H. Ivey was born in 1844. In September 1861, he enlisted in Company E, 10th Florida Infantry CSA in Sumterville, Sumter County. He was captured at Petersburg, Virginia, and sent to Point Lookout Prison in Maryland. In 1873, Ivey married Mary Bequick; around 1919, they moved to Kissimmee. He died on July 14, 1924, and is buried at Shingle Creek Cemetery. (Courtesy of the Osceola County Historical Society.)

Morgan Bonaparte "Bone" Mizell was Florida's quintessential "cracker cowboy." Born in Horse Creek, Florida, in 1863, his siblings included Confederate veterans, lawmen, and judges. In 1895, artist Frederic Remington depicted Mizell in a painting, *A Cracker Cowboy*. Mizell was described as being "an expert horseman, crack shot with rifle and six-gun, lightning fast with a bullwhip, rope and branding iron." (Courtesy of the Osceola County Historical Society.)

Lawrence Silas was made famous by writer Zora Neale Hurston, who, in a 1942 *Saturday Evening Post* article, called him "Lawrence of the River," referring to the Kissimmee River region, where Silas owned thousands of acres. His father, Tom Silas, a former slave, came to Florida after the War Between the States and established the first school for black students in what is now Osceola County. (Courtesy of the Osceola County Historical Society.)

Alfred Sydney Campbell enlisted in Tampa in March 1862 and was assigned to Capt. James Gettis's Company, Gates Division, 7th Florida Regiment CSA. Campbell was soon promoted to second sergeant and participated in 13 major battles. He became a Florida cattleman after the war. Campbell was married twice; he had 10 children with his first wife. He passed away in West Palm Beach. (Courtesy of the Osceola County Historical Society.)

The Bass family was one of Osceola's pioneer families. Confederate veteran George Washington Bass, born in Georgia in 1844, was married to Susanna Sansbury of North Carolina. They raised seven children in a home they built at the corner of Main and Oak Streets in Kissimmee in 1882. Bass died in 1914 and is buried in Rose Hill Cemetery. (Courtesy of the Osceola County Historical Society.)

Born in 1844, Hamilton Disston was a wealthy industrialist. During the war, he formed the "Disston Volunteers" in Philadelphia with workers from the Disston factory. In 1881, he purchased four million acres of land from the State of Florida, bailing the state out of debt and becoming the largest single landowner in the United States at that time. Disston operated a sugar mill in St. Cloud. (Courtesy of State Archives of Florida.)

Louis Napoleon Nelson fought with Company M, 7th Tennessee Cavalry under the command of Gen. Nathan Bedford Forrest. Nelson participated in many battles, including Vicksburg. He accompanied his master's sons to war, serving as a cook, rifleman, and chaplain. Nelson attended 39 Confederate reunions wearing his uniform. This 1932 photograph features Nelson with grandson Nelson Winbush, who became an educator and member of the Sons of Confederate Veterans. (Courtesy of Nelson Winbush.)

In 1909, the Seminole Land and Investment Company (SLICO) of Washington, DC, purchased 35,000 acres of the old Hamilton Disston sugar plantation to build a retirement community for Union veterans. In April 1909, William G. King, an estate manager in Alachua County before becoming the first resident of St. Cloud, was chosen to plan, locate, and develop the community. In May 1909, a corps of surveyors (above) was employed to lay out the new town of St. Cloud. The Grand Army of the Republic Association sold the first 100 five-acre lots for $50 each. The settlement was home to the largest concentration of Union veterans in the South, second only to Chicago in the nation. William G. King Real Estate in St. Cloud (left) served as the agent for SLICO. (Both, courtesy of the Osceola County Historical Society.)

George S. Burtner served as a corporal in Company F, 61st Illinois Infantry Regiment USA, which was organized at Carrollton, Illinois, in February 1862. Burtner saw action in many battles, including Shiloh, Vicksburg, and Franklin. He is pictured here with his wife, Jennie, on the porch of their new St. Cloud home, which he built in 1910. Their daughter, Ethel, is seated at right. The woman at left is unidentified. (Courtesy of the Osceola County Historical Society.)

This early 1900s photograph shows the Grand Army of the Republic Patriots' Day parade on New York Avenue in St. Cloud. GAR camps from all over the country participated, including the Ulysses Simpson Grant Post No. 28 from Chicago. Patriots' Day was first proclaimed in 1894 to commemorate the battles of Lexington and Concord and, later, the first bloodshed of the War Between the States. (Courtesy of the Osceola County Historical Society.)

Lucius L. Mitchell, born in 1846, served in Company D, 35th Kentucky Infantry. On December 4, 1909, he became the first Union veteran to die in the St. Cloud soldiers' colony. On January 4, 1910, the Lucius L. Mitchell GAR Post No. 34 in St. Cloud was chartered under the Department of Florida. Mitchell is buried in Mount Peace Cemetery. (Courtesy of the St. Cloud Heritage Museum.)

The Louis L. Mitchell GAR Post No. 34 Fife and Drum Corps is seen in front of the Grand Army of the Republic Memorial Hall on Massachusetts Avenue in St. Cloud, preparing to march in the annual veterans' reunion parade. This photograph was taken around 1915. (Courtesy of the St. Cloud Heritage Museum.)

The GAR Memorial Hall is located on Massachusetts Avenue. It was built in 1914 by three of the Allied Orders of the GAR then established in St. Cloud: Lucius L. Mitchell GAR Post No. 34, Woman's Relief Corps No. 12, and the Sons of Veterans No. 8 Abraham Lincoln Camp. On February 21, 1997, it was listed in the National Register of Historic Places. (Courtesy of Alma Nevarez Grenier.)

This GAR monument is located at the corner of New York Avenue and Thirteenth Street in St. Cloud. It was erected in 2000 in Veterans Park to honor the Union veterans who were the founders of St. Cloud, Florida's "Wonder City." This monument, though it has a different inscription, is a replica of the historic monument located in Mount Peace Cemetery. (Courtesy of Alma Nevarez Grenier.)

Amzi Davis Harmon was born on April 18, 1845, in Westmoreland County, Pennsylvania. A corporal in Company K, 211th Pennsylvania Infantry, Harmon was the recipient of the Medal of Honor for heroism in capturing a flag on April 2, 1865, at Petersburg, Virginia. The medal was issued on May 20, 1865. Harmon died on October 9, 1927, and is buried in Mount Peace Cemetery. (Courtesy of Alma Nevarez Grenier.)

The Battle of Narcoossee Mill is presented by Jacob Summerlin Camp No. 1516, Sons of Confederate Veterans. The reenactment is held annually at Ralph V. Chisholm Park in St. Cloud. Shown here are members of Company B, 17th Connecticut Volunteer Infantry. They are, from left to right, (first row) Daryl Mercado and Jeff Grzelak; (second row) Larry Jakab, Mark Barber, Bobby Wyatt, Bob Grenier, Rusty Grenier, and Glenn Cremeans. (Photograph by and courtesy of Larry Jakab.)

Three

Sumter and Lake
Introducing the Sweet Orange

Sumter County, named for Revolutionary War general Thomas Sumter, was established on January 8, 1853. Lake County, created from parts of Orange and Sumter, was established on May 27, 1887. The name was suggested by Confederate veteran Henry Duncan because of the estimated 1,400 lakes within its boundaries. Pictured here in 1908 are 22 Confederate veterans at a reunion picnic at the Linden Cemetery in Sumter County. (Courtesy of State Archives of Florida.)

John Cabell Breckinridge served four years as vice president under James Buchanan. During the war, Breckinridge served as a Confederate general. In the closing months of the war in 1865, Jefferson Davis appointed Breckinridge his secretary of war. Following the conflict, Breckinridge eluded capture and fled to Florida, making a stop in Oxford before sailing to Cuba. He returned to the United States in 1869. (Courtesy of State Archives of Florida.)

Peter Boyer Perry and his wife, Elizabeth, tended a farm at Oxford. Perry, a heroic flag-bearer during the Mexican-American War, served in Company E, 9th Florida Infantry CSA. During his 18-month service, he fought at Cold Harbor, Petersburg, and Olustee. After the surrender, Perry walked home to Florida. In the 1870s, he moved his family a few miles west, to a scrub area he called Pedro. (Courtesy of Bob Lovell.)

Capt. David Hume Baker was born in McLean County, Kentucky, on October 7, 1841. In 1862, he was commissioned first lieutenant in Company F, 12th Kentucky Cavalry. Baker married Mary Hannah of Elizabethtown. He served Kentucky as a state senator from 1873 to 1875, representing Muhlenberg County. In 1886, the Bakers moved to Florida, where David grew oranges. He served on the Sumter County commission and as a state senator representing Sumter and Marion Counties. Baker was a director of Munroe & Chambliss National Bank in Ocala, which opened in 1914. He died on June 1, 1917, at Orange Home (below) and was buried with military honors in Arlington National Cemetery in Virginia. His son, David M. Baker, died shortly thereafter, in July 1917. (Both, courtesy of the Wildwood Area Historical Association.)

In 1845, Melton Haynes settled near Leesburg, where he and his brother Bunberry planted a quarter-acre of "sweet orange" seeds. This planting gave birth to the region's citrus industry. In 1849, he married Sarah Isabella Vaught in Palatka. Haynes was captain of Company H, 5th Battalion Florida Cavalry. He served in the Florida State House of Representatives and in the Florida Senate. Haynes died on January 10, 1883. (Artwork by and courtesy of Bob Grenier Sr.)

Born on July 18, 1821, John Marmaduke Robertson arrived at Lake Griffin in August 1843. He served in Capt. Haynes's Company H, 5th Battalion, 2nd Florida Cavalry. In 1854, he settled the community of Whitney, near Leesburg. Robertson was married to Mary Ellen Morrison and then to Mary Ann Permelia Ward. In 1868, he was a charter member of the Leesburg Masonic Lodge. (Courtesy of Leesburg Masonic Lodge No. 58.)

In 1862, Albert D. Wright mustered into the Union army as a sergeant in Company A, 49th Pennsylvania Volunteer Infantry. In April 1864, he became captain of Company D, 43rd US Colored Troops. Wright was awarded the Medal of Honor in 1893 for his actions at the Battle of the Crater, where he was wounded capturing a stand of colors. He is buried in Eustis. (Artwork by and courtesy of Bob Grenier Sr.)

Maj. Alexander St. Clair Abrams was born on March 10, 1845, in New Orleans. He served as a private in Company A, Withers' Light Artillery. In 1863, he was captured at the Siege of Vicksburg. He founded the city of Tavares, Florida, in 1880. He died in Jacksonville on June 5, 1931, after a brilliant career as a soldier, lawyer, newspaper editor, and public servant. (Artwork by and courtesy of Bob Grenier Sr.)

Capt. Montgomery G. Cooper served in the 10th Iowa Infantry. The regiment fought in campaigns that included the Siege of Vicksburg, the Battle of Chattanooga, and Sherman's "March to the Sea." In 1885, Cooper moved with his wife, Alice, and their three children to Clermont. He donated land in 1914 to build Clermont's first library, which is named the Cooper Memorial Library in his honor. (Courtesy of Chief Carle Bishop.)

George Thomas King enlisted in the US Navy in Boston in 1863, serving aboard the gunboat *Nipsic*, the side-wheel steamer *Mahaska*, and the warship *Ohio*. In 1884, King traveled to today's south Lake County and purchased 900 acres, where he began plotting a town and building the King "villa," the first in what would become Villa City. King and his wife, Emma, had three children. (Courtesy of Howard King.)

Thomas Hux served in the 18th Artillery Battalion, also known as Manigault's Artillery Battalion and the South Carolina Siege Train. In 1869, Hux settled in Fort Mason, where he married Mary Ballard. In 1872, they homesteaded land south of Tavares, raising sugarcane and oranges. The town of Astatula was established from land owned by Hux. In 1912, they moved to Tavares. Hux died in 1939. (Courtesy of Judy Hux Rainey.)

John Milton Bryan, a native of Hamilton County, served as a scout during the Third Seminole War (1855–1858). He was an officer in the Madison Gray Eagles of the Third Florida Infantry. In addition, Bryan was an orange grower, state senator, state representative, and member of the first railroad commission. In 1867, Bryan married Louisa Margaret Norton, and the couple settled in Umatilla. (Courtesy of the Lake County Historical Society.)

Dennis "Pop" Mike arrived in Leesburg from South Carolina in 1860. His original name was Dennis Dickey, but when he was freed, he changed his last name to Mike, after his former owner's son. He lived to the age of 110 years and 11 months. His wife, Priscilla, a midwife, delivered many of Leesburg's early residents. In 1928, Mike Street was named for the family. (Courtesy of the Leesburg Heritage Society.)

Daniel Shipman Troy (second from right) was a lieutenant colonel for the 60th Alabama Infantry. In 1862, Troy was wounded leading a charge at Drewry's Bluff, Virginia. He was captured and nursed back to health in a Union hospital. In the 1880s, Troy built a home at Lane Park called Oxmoor. Troy's wife is seated at center, wearing the dark bonnet. (Courtesy of the Lake County Historical Society.)

Marian D. Duncan, the daughter of Henry Holcomb Duncan and Marian Peet Duncan, is a highlight of this photograph of Lake County Confederate veterans, taken at the Pioneer Building in Tavares in the 1890s. Henry Duncan, standing to Marian's left, served in Company C, 45th Alabama Infantry. Sgt. Thomas Kennedy Hall (first row, fourth from left) served with Company E, 3rd Georgia Volunteers. (Courtesy of the Lake County Historical Society.)

On March 29, 1895, members of the United Confederate Veterans and Union veterans of the Grand Army of the Republic pose with the Leesburg Rifles at a reenactment for Chautauqua entertainment. The encampment was held on grounds between Mount Dora and Tavares. Henry Holcomb Duncan, a two-term Florida Division commander of the UCV, is standing third from left. (Courtesy of State Archives of Florida.)

Cpl. Ens. Marshal Smith served in Company K, 34th Massachusetts Infantry. In 1864, Smith was severely wounded through the lung and foot at New Market, Virginia. He lay in a gully for two days before being rescued by a woman. Imprisoned by the Confederates, he later escaped and walked 95 miles north to Federal lines. He was present at the surrender at Appomattox. (Courtesy of Don Polly and Edward Caputo.)

Renaud Prosper Landry was second lieutenant of the Donaldsonville Volunteer Battery, also known as the "Cannoneers of Donaldsonville," which was organized in Louisiana in August 1861. He was promoted to captain in 1864. The battery was present at Second Manassas, Antietam, Gettysburg, Petersburg, and Lee's surrender at Appomattox Court House. On February 16, 1855, Prosper married Adele Pedesclaux at Ascension Catholic Church in Donaldsonville. (Courtesy of Victor E. Smith III.)

As shown in the above photograph, on April 26, 1935, a memorial fountain was dedicated to the soldiers from all wars who are laid to rest in Lone Oak Cemetery. Fannie Ezell, the president of Lone Oak Cemetery Inc. and the secretary of Confederate Gray Chapter No. 641, United Daughters of the Confederacy, directed the service. Chapter No. 641 was founded on December 31, 1902. Florida Statute 683.01 (j) commemorates April 26, the anniversary of Gen. Joseph Johnston's surrender to Gen. William Sherman in Durham, North Carolina, in 1865, as Confederate Memorial Day. Each year on April 26, the chapter holds a memorial service at the fountain in Lone Oak Cemetery. In 2013, members of the Sons of Confederate Veterans joined the United Daughters of the Confederacy for the 110th Confederate Memorial Day ceremony at Lone Oak Cemetery (below). (Above, courtesy of the Leesburg Heritage Society; below, courtesy of Sanda Crabtree Mott.)

Members of the Marion Dragoons UDC Chapter No. 2311 of Weirsdale gather around the Oxford Confederate Veterans monument at Pine Level Cemetery. The cemetery, located in Oxford, was established in 1865. From left to right are June Fulmer Dunn, Jaca Ross Mills, Gwen Hughes Britt, Judy Hux Rainey, Robbie Mason Jinks, Norma Perry Bowles, Sanda Crabtree Mott, Mary Ann White Langford, and Carol Cason Mathews. (Courtesy of Sanda Crabtree Mott.)

In September 2013, the inaugural "Rifles, Rails & History: Steam Back to the North and South" Living History Encampment took place at Wooton Park in Tavares. The event, conceived by Heather Graham, included the Orange Blossom Cannonball "movie train" featured in the television miniseries *North and South* and *The Blue and the Gray*; a replica of the Confederate submarine *H.L. Hunley*; and a Robert E. Lee portrayer, Al Stone. (Courtesy of Brian Whicher and Roberta Simms.)

Four

SEMINOLE COUNTY
SANFORD, CELERY, AND THE SENATOR

Seminole County, named for descendants of the Creek people, was established on April 25, 1913. After the great freeze of 1895, Sanford, the county seat, rebuilt its economy with celery, becoming known as "Celery City." Seminole is home to The Senator, once the biggest and oldest cypress tree in the world. Pictured here is veteran and Geneva pioneer Andrew Holder, who served in Company D, 45th Georgia Infantry. (Courtesy of the Geneva Historical Society.)

In 1861, Henry Shelton Sanford was appointed by Pres. Abraham Lincoln as US minister to Belgium. Sanford coordinated Secret Service operations during the war and arranged for the purchase of war materials for the Union. While a diplomat, he attempted to prevent the South from gaining support from European nations. After the war, Sanford purchased 23 square miles of land south of Lake Monroe, much of it coming from Confederate general Joseph Finegan. He established a slaughterhouse, sawmill, general store, and hotel in the 1870s. It was in this area that he founded the city that bears his name. His wealth and political and personal influence helped develop Central Florida. In 1864, he married Gertrude Ellen Dupuy in Paris, France. Sanford died at Healing Springs, Virginia, on May 21, 1891, and is buried in Connecticut. (Left, courtesy of Sanford Museum; right, courtesy of the Library of Congress.)

Edward Warren Henck, a Union officer, served with the honor guard that accompanied Pres. Abraham Lincoln's body on the train trip from Washington to Illinois. In 1872, Henck arrived in Orange County from Boston. In 1876, he established Longwood, naming it after a fashionable Boston suburb, and served as the first postmaster. After Longwood was incorporated in 1883, Henck was elected its first mayor. (Courtesy of Central Florida Society for Historical Preservation.)

Confederate veteran John Neill Searcy served from May 1861 to May 1865 in Hudson's Battery, Mississippi Light Artillery, also known as the Pettus Flying Artillery. At the age of 31, he traveled from Tennessee by the side-wheel steamer *Starlight*, arriving at Mellonville on Lake Monroe on March 23, 1873. Searcy married Eva Lessie Muzzy in 1885 and died in Longwood on October 27, 1926. (Courtesy of Central Florida Society for Historical Preservation.)

James Hiram Lee was the first lieutenant of Company E, 10th Florida Infantry. The 10th was formed in 1864 from companies of the 1st and 2nd Florida Infantry Battalions. In 1867, Lee married Laura Barnett, and in 1874, the couple moved to the Lake Jessup settlement. Lee is pictured here in 1885 with his sisters-in-law Julia and Della Barnett (far left) and four of his nine children. (Courtesy of Oviedo Historical Society.)

William Lockett, pictured here at his grove in Geneva, was born in Forsyth, Georgia, in April 1841. He enlisted at Macon in Company D, 2nd Georgia Infantry Battalion. Lockett performed many duties during his service, including special duty for Gen. Benjamin Huger, as well as a wagon and forage master. In 1863, he was promoted to quartermaster sergeant. Lockett was married to Lula Hammond. (Courtesy of the Geneva Historical Society.)

Alexander R. Niblo was born in Montgomery County, Pennsylvania, in 1828. Niblo, a plasterer by trade, enlisted in the Union army at Salem, Ohio, in 1862 and was mustered into Company G, 104th Ohio Infantry Regiment at Camp Massillon. He was promoted to corporal in 1863. Niblo was married to Frances Bucher and lived in Geneva. He died on November 13, 1904. (Courtesy of the Geneva Historical Society.)

Dr. Daniel Pattishall attended medical school in Philadelphia. In November 1859, he married Georgia Brown. On May 16, 1862, Pattishall was assigned to Company K, 62nd Georgia Infantry, but was discharged the same day. In March 1864, he was commissioned second lieutenant in the Dooly County Militia. Pattishall also served in the 6th and 7th Georgia Militia. In 1889, the Pattishalls moved to Geneva. (Courtesy of the Geneva Historical Society.)

In the 1880s, Robert A. Mills arrived from Iowa and developed the Chuluota community, where he opened a sawmill and raised cattle. *Chuluota* was a Creek word meaning "pine island," a name Mills chose because the settlement was located along a lake dotted with islands of pine. Mills is pictured wearing his Grand Army of the Republic medal with a captain's suspension bar. (Courtesy of the Seminole County Historical Society.)

Joseph Nathaniel Crooms's parents were slaves on a Tallahassee plantation. From 1906 to 1926, Crooms served as the principal of Hopper Academy in Sanford's Georgetown neighborhood. Hopper dates back to 1886, when it was called Colored School No. 11. In 1926, Crooms established and was principal of Crooms Academy, the county's first black high school. His wife, Wealthy Mabel, was the assistant principal. (Courtesy of the Seminole County Student Museum.)

Henry Baker (fourth from left) is seen here in the 1890s with Geneva-area orange growers. Born in 1840 in Orange County, Virginia, Baker served as a lieutenant in Company D, 19th Virginia Infantry. In 1865, he was captured and imprisoned at Johnson's Island, Ohio. A widower living with his daughter Mary in Geneva, Baker filed for a Confederate's pension claim in June 1915. (Courtesy of the Geneva Historical Society.)

William Selby Harney was born in 1800 in Tennessee. He distinguished himself in the Black Hawk, Florida, and Mexican-American Wars. In 1855, Harney was on frontier assignment when he defeated the Sioux Indians at Sand Hills. He retired in 1863 and died in Orlando in 1899. He is buried in Arlington National Cemetery with his wife, Mary Elizabeth. Lake Harney near Geneva is named for him. (Courtesy of State Archives of Florida.)

Lewis Thornton Powell moved with his family to Live Oak in 1859. He served in Company I, 2nd Florida Infantry, known as the "Hamilton Blues." He was wounded and captured at Gettysburg. In October 1863, Powell escaped from a Union hospital and joined Mosby's Rangers. He conspired with John Wilkes Booth to assassinate President Lincoln, Vice Pres. Andrew Johnson, Secretary of State William Seward, and General Grant. Powell attacked Seward with a knife, but Seward survived. Powell, tried under the name Lewis Payne, was hung with Mary Surratt, David Herold, and George Atzerodt on July 7, 1865. On November 12, 1994, Powell's great-grandniece, Helen Alderman (below), interred Powell's remains in the Geneva Cemetery. The remains included Powell's skull, which had arrived from the Smithsonian Institution a few days earlier. (Left, courtesy of the Geneva Historical Society; below, courtesy of Jim Robison.)

Five

Orange County
Condado de los Mosquitos

Orange County was established on December 29, 1824, from a segment of St. Johns County. It was originally called Mosquito County, after the name the Spanish had given the Florida coast, Los Mosquitos. In January 1845, the Territorial Council approved the name change to Orange County, after all the orange groves that were rapidly being planted throughout the region. Pictured here are Confederate veterans in Orlando in November 1920. (Author's collection.)

Jacob Summerlin earned his fortune raising cattle. During the war, he was a blockade runner who smuggled beef and medicine to Confederate troops from Live Oak Point. With his financial support, Summerlin helped Bartow become the county seat of Polk County, where he established the Summerlin Institute. In 1875, he succeeded in defeating his rival, Henry Sanford, in making Orlando the county seat of Orange County. (Courtesy of State Archives of Florida.)

David Mizell was born in 1833 near Lake City, and in 1854, he married Angeline Augusta May in Newnansville. They moved to Orange County in 1858, following the Third Seminole War. In 1862, he joined Jonathan Stewart's Company G, 8th Florida Volunteers. In 1868, Gov. Harrison Reed appointed Mizell sheriff of Orange County. In 1870, on his way to arrest Moses Barber, Mizell was shot and killed. (Courtesy of State Archives of Florida.)

Bluford Marion Sims was born in Marietta, Georgia, in 1836. In March 1864, he became second lieutenant of Company B, Walker's Battalion, Thomas's North Carolina Legion. In August 1865, Sims headed to Orange County and settled at Fuller's Crossing. He led a group in platting a town that, in 1886, would be called Ocoee. Sims was a teacher, builder, and citrus-industry innovator. (Courtesy of Violet Sims and Mike Everhart.)

Philadelphian Thomas Ellwood Zell served as the captain of Company A, 121st Pennsylvania Volunteers. He mustered out with the rank of lieutenant colonel. Zell cofounded the Military Order of the Loyal Legion, which was established upon news of Lincoln's assassination. Zellwood is named for him, and Lake Maggiore is named for his wife. Zell was a publisher best known for his 1876 *Atlas for the United States Centennial.* (Artwork by and courtesy of Andrew Peterson.)

Robert Ivey was born in 1848 in Hamilton County. In 1857, his family moved to Orange County, where they homesteaded 640 acres near Lake Eola. Ivey enlisted at Fort Reed in 1864 and served in the Cow Cavalry under Capt. W.B. Watson. In 1869, he married Mary Lovica Brown in Orlando. After Mary's death in 1888 he moved to Polk County, where, in 1912, he married Nancy Harrelson Spivery. (Courtesy of Sheila McMullen Tindle.)

Charles B. Lin of Atlanta was a second corporal in Company B Battalion, Georgia Military Institute Cadets, located in Marietta, which saw service in the Confederate army from May 10, 1864, to May 20, 1865. The cadets entered service against the Union along the Chattahoochee River in July 1864. This 1888 photograph shows Lin with his wife, Ida Brown, and children, Carl and Ruth Ann. (Courtesy of the Apopka Historical Society.)

Zelotes H. Mason was born in 1814 in Philadelphia. He moved to Florida in the 1850s and served as a surgeon in the Florida Home Guard. He and his wife, Christiana, arrived in the Apopka area in 1871. Mason was also an orange planter and assisted in securing Apopka's charter. In 1883, he was Grand Master of the Free and Accepted Masons of Florida. (Courtesy of the Apopka Historical Society.)

Sylvanus M. Hankins was born on January 15, 1846. He joined Company D, 11th Florida Infantry at Madison County in June 1864 and served under Capt. John Bryan. The 11th Florida was sent to Virginia and attached to Finegan's Brigade. Hankins married Elizabeth Stubbs in Orange County on December 24, 1888. He died on August 9, 1918, and is buried at Woodlawn Cemetery in Tampa. (Courtesy of State Archives of Florida.)

George Horatio Packwood was a New York native who served as a lieutenant in the Union army. The trefoil badge he is wearing indicates he fought in the Second Corps. After the war, Packwood lived in Louisiana. In the early 1870s, he and his brother, Dr. Richard Packwood, settled near Lake Maitland. Packwood filed the first plat for the town of Maitland in September 1881. (Courtesy of the Maitland Historical Society.)

This historical marker, cosponsored by the Apopka Historical Society, indicates the site where, in 1872, William A. Lovell purchased 225 acres of land to be used as a hub for freight service and commerce on Lake Apopka and the surrounding region. The marker is located at Magnolia Park in Apopka. Lovell served in Company H, 5th Battalion, 2nd Florida Cavalry, under the command of Capt. Melton Haynes. (Author's collection.)

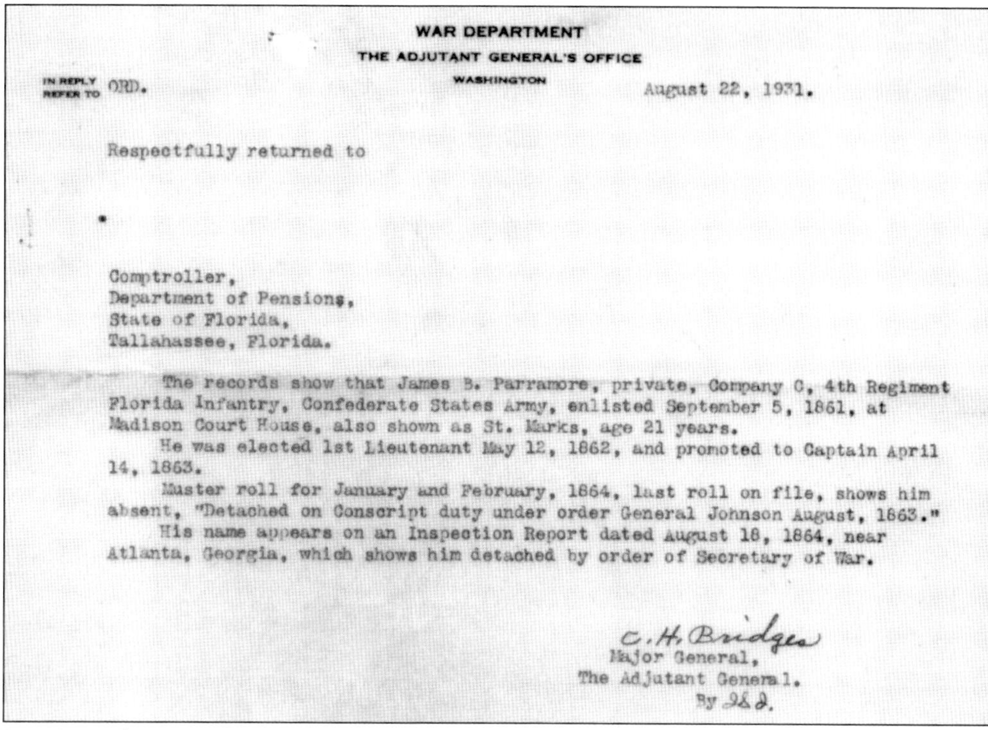

WAR DEPARTMENT
THE ADJUTANT GENERAL'S OFFICE
WASHINGTON

IN REPLY REFER TO ORD.

August 22, 1931.

Respectfully returned to

Comptroller,
Department of Pensions,
State of Florida,
Tallahassee, Florida.

The records show that James B. Parramore, private, Company C, 4th Regiment Florida Infantry, Confederate States Army, enlisted September 5, 1861, at Madison Court House, also shown as St. Marks, age 21 years.

He was elected 1st Lieutenant May 12, 1862, and promoted to Captain April 14, 1863.

Muster roll for January and February, 1864, last roll on file, shows him absent, "Detached on Conscript duty under order General Johnson August, 1863."

His name appears on an Inspection Report dated August 18, 1864, near Atlanta, Georgia, which shows him detached by order of Secretary of War.

C. H. Bridges
Major General,
The Adjutant General.
By [illegible]

In 1931, Leila Long Parramore filed for a pension claim as the widow of Capt. James B. Parramore. Born in Thomasville, Georgia, in 1840, James Parramore enlisted in 1861 and served in Company C, 4th Florida Infantry. He was elected first lieutenant in May 1862 and then captain in April 1863. Parramore served as Orlando mayor from 1896 to 1902, passing away while in office. (Courtesy of State Archives of Florida.)

At the onset of the war, when President Lincoln called for 75,000 volunteers to serve for three months, Mahlon Gore joined the 2nd Michigan Infantry. In 1861, Gore and his wife, Josephine, moved to Iowa, and then to the Dakota Territory. They moved to Orlando around 1880, where Gore purchased the *Orange County Reporter* and served as mayor. Gore died in 1916 and is buried in Orlando's Greenwood Cemetery. (Author's collection.)

In 1862, Loring Augustus Chase enlisted in a Massachusetts regiment and served nine months, working garrison duty in North Carolina. In 1881, he and Oliver Chapman purchased 700 acres of land to establish what would become Winter Park. Chase spent the remainder of his life establishing the city. Chase, who died in 1906, left his estate to Rollins College. (Courtesy of Rollins College Archives.)

In 1845, Francis Bangs Knowles began to manufacture men's clothing and gloves in New York. During the war, the Union army commissioned him to make gloves for the soldiers. Knowles moved to Winter Park in 1885 and became a director of the Winter Park Land Company. He made significant contributions to Winter Park and Rollins College. He died in Washington, DC, on May 15, 1890. (Courtesy of Rollins College Archives.)

Franklin Fairbanks, pictured here with his wife, Frances, in 1852, served as a colonel on the staffs of Vermont governors Hiland Hall and Erastus Fairbanks. Fairbanks was responsible for raising, equipping, and training troops during the war. He came to Winter Park around 1881 and played a huge role in establishing Florida's postwar vacation-home construction industry. He was one of the first trustees of Winter Park's Rollins College. (Courtesy of Rollins College Archives.)

Will Wallace Harney was the editor of the *Louisville Journal* in Kentucky. The governor offered him a colonelcy during the war, but Harney declined. In 1868, he and his wife, Mary, came to Orlando and homesteaded on Lake Conway. Mary died soon after. In 1874, Harney built a house of pine that he dubbed Pine Castle (pictured). The community that grew around him became known by that name. (Artwork by and courtesy of Shirley Cannon.)

In 1854, William P. Delk moved from Georgia to Florida with his family and settled near Rock Springs. The family farmed and operated a gristmill, sawmill, and cotton gin. In May 1862, Delk enlisted with Capt. Jonathan Stewart's Company G, 8th Florida Infantry Regiment. He died from disease on July 15, 1862, in Tallahassee. Delk is buried in the Old Church Cemetery in Apopka. (Courtesy of the Apopka Historical Society.)

Byron Peavy, great-grandnephew of Confederate cavalry captain Melton Haynes, is a fifth-generation Floridian raised in Ocoee. Peavy is the captain of Company D, 10th Tennessee reenactors and an officer in the Florida Division Sons of Confederate Veterans. He and his wife, Catherine, are Southern heritage preservationists. Peavy is pictured riding Diablo, his award-winning paint quarter horse. Diablo died on December 1, 2013. (Courtesy of Kristy Lennon.)

Six

Volusia, the Lighthouse Keeper, and the Sugar Mill

Volusia County was established on December 29, 1854. It took its name from Volusia, one of Florida's oldest settlements, located on the east bank of the St. Johns River, across from Astor. There are several theories as to the name's origin. Pictured is Confederate captain Edward Camden in 1917. On the first day of World War I, he put on his uniform and tried to enlist. (Courtesy of State Archives of Florida.)

William R. Rowlinski, shown at left with his wife, Mary, was born in 1833 in Russia and immigrated to South Carolina when he was 17. In April 1862, Rowlinski joined Company A, 24th South Carolina Infantry. He saw action at Chickamauga and in the Atlanta campaign, where he was captured and sent to Camp Douglas Prison in Chicago. Rowlinski joined the US Lighthouse Service in 1883 and was assigned to the St. Augustine Light Station. On October 1, 1887, he was appointed acting keeper at the newly constructed Mosquito Inlet Lighthouse (now the Ponce Inlet Lighthouse, seen at right in the below photograph) in Volusia County. On November 1, 1887, he became the first person to illuminate the kerosene lantern. At left in the below photograph, William and Mary Rowlinski are seen in retirement in the early 1900s. (Left, courtesy of the Rowlinski family collection; below, courtesy of Ponce Inlet Lighthouse Station.)

Descendants of William Rowlinski, upon finding his gravesite unmarked, requested the assistance of the Sons of Confederate Veterans in obtaining a military headstone. On July 16, 2005, a dedication for the new monument took place at the Edgewater New Smyrna Cemetery. Rowlinski's great-granddaughter, Roberta Pacetti Rothrock, pictured at right in 1932, requested that a poem she wrote in the 1950s be read at the ceremony. She was 94 when the dedication was held. Rothrock died in 2007. Below, Bob Grenier (left) and Paul Arthur Mott serve as the color guard at the dedication. Mott died on September 18, 2010, and is buried at the Florida National Cemetery in Bushnell. He was a World War II and Korean War veteran and a member of the Sons of Confederate Veterans. (Right, courtesy of the Rowlinski family collection; left, courtesy of Sanda Crabtree Mott.)

Fifth Battalion Florida Cavalry

Company H

Officers

Commissioned

M. Haynes, Captain
Thos. E. Haile, First Lieutenant
B.F.S. Brantly, Second Lieutenant

Non-Commission

SERGEANTS

J. M. Bryen, First Sergeant
S. A. Curry, Second Sergeant
B. E. Dupont, Third Sergeant
J. M. Hardy, Fourth Sergeant
J. Starke, Fifth Sergeant

CORPORALS

J. M. Thomas, First Corporal
J. W. Fussell, Second Corporal
W. G. Rowland, Third Corporal
N. Davis, Fourth Corporal

MUSICIAN

E. H. Crowe, Musician

PRIVATES

Adams, R. J.
Bennett, D. L.
Brooks, R.
Brooks, J. D.
Brantley, W.
Bryan, W.
Caldwell, F.S.
Collins, H.
Colter, A.
Chalker, J. B.
Crane, H.
Davis, E. G.
Davis, W. A.
Dial, G.
Drawdy, D.
Dupont, J.B.
Eleriber, R.P.
Fort, A.
Fort, J.
Griffin, B.
Gough, J. E.
Grantham, D.
Haile, J. C.
Harper, F.
Hart, C. C.
Hart, J.D.
Hull, E. J.
Jones, J.
Kirley, H. J

PRIVATES

Lovell, W.A.
Meddow, A. N.
Meddow, J.
Marsh, R.
Nesbet, T. G.
Newman, M. M.
Parish, J. A.
Peters, A. H.
Peters, G. H.
Perry, A. H.
Piles, T. S.
Rawlems, J.
Rawlems, W. H.
Robertson, S. M.
Robertson, R.
Rogers, M. H.
Sligh, J. M.
Sligh, S. P.
Smith, P.
Sturmans, W. D.
Tillman, J. B.
Thompson, John
Tucker, W. J.
Vaught, A.
Wofford, J. T.
Ward, W. J.
Whidden, J.
Yates, J. B.
Young, J. B.

On October 15, 1863, the 5th Battalion, 2nd Florida Cavalry was organized at the Volusia settlement. The battalion's Company H was assigned to Capt. J.J. Dickison's command. James Starke served as the company's captain, but he soon resigned, giving command to 1st Lt. Melton Haynes. In December 1864, Lt. Thomas Haile transferred into "Melton's Marvels." Haynes was promoted to captain on January 23, 1865. (Artwork by and courtesy of Bob Grenier Sr.)

Ed Beckett (left) and Moses Marsh (right) from Ocala mustered into Company C, 2nd Florida Cavalry in 1861. They fought at Olustee, Gainesville, and Braddock's Farm. Marsh and his brothers were early settlers of Volusia County. He ran cattle, farmed, and worked as a butcher in DeLand. Marsh died on April 29, 1892, and is buried in the Beresford Presbyterian Cemetery near Lake Beresford, west of DeLand. (Courtesy of Tom Roberts.)

In 1861, John Donaghy enlisted in Company B, 12th Pennsylvania Infantry, Duquesne Greys. He then joined Company F, 103rd Pennsylvania Infantry, and became company captain. He was taken prisoner in North Carolina and sent to Andersonville Prison, escaping six months later. Donaghy, a well-known artist, moved to DeLand on Lake Winnemissett in 1880. In 1926, he wrote a book about his war experiences. (Courtesy of Tom Roberts.)

Union general William Birney was born in Alabama in 1819. In 1864, he led a 10-day raid through Volusia County. "Birney's Raid" was the last major attempt by Union forces in Florida to overcome the February defeat at Olustee. Birney disrupted Confederate supply lines in Volusia and destroyed supply sources, including Thomas Starke's Spring Garden Plantation. Riverboats were destroyed, prisoners and horses taken, and slaves liberated. (Courtesy of the Library of Congress.)

The spring-run sugar mill at DeLeon Springs, and the mill's waterwheel, were built around 1832 by Col. Orlando Rees, the owner of Spring Garden Plantation. The mill was destroyed in 1836 during the Second Seminole War. Thomas Starke traded 50 slaves for the property rights to the plantation and rebuilt it in the 1840s. Starke utilized his mill to aid the Confederacy through most of the War Between the States, and the site became a target for retaliation by Union forces. Gen. William Birney, during his 1864 raid though Volusia, destroyed the mill. Above, visitors to the springs in the 1890s climb the disabled waterwheel. Below, tourists visit the mill in the 1880s. Today, the mill is a popular restaurant called the Old Spanish Sugar Mill, which was opened in 1961 by Marjorie and Peter Schwarze. (Both, courtesy of West Volusia Historical Society.)

John Anderson Bradley Jr. was born in 1842 in Chester, South Carolina. In 1861, he left his studies at The Citadel and enlisted in Company A, 2nd South Carolina Cavalry, Hampton's Legion. In a recommendation letter, Maj. Gen. M.C. Butler called Bradley a "faithful and gallant soldier of the Confederate States Army." After the war, Bradley completed his studies and began his law career. He moved to Georgia and married Mary Lucinda Davis in December 1874. The couple had eight children. In 1885 they moved to Florida, settling at Enterprise, where Bradley served as mayor. The Bradleys later moved to Deland, where he served as justice of the peace and as deputy clerk. John Bradley, an active member of the United Confederate Veterans, died on December 1, 1910. (Both, courtesy of Lisa Glass Stanley, Sharon Bradley Malloy, and John W. Bradley.)

Frank W. Sams, pictured with his wife, Zelia (center), and daughter, Anna, was born at Palatka in 1846. In 1861, he enlisted in Company F, 3rd Florida Infantry, known as "Duval's Cowboys." Sams moved to New Smyrna in 1868 and became a cattle rancher. In 1887, he served on the first town council of New Smyrna and as mayor. He was a Florida state senator from 1899 to 1909. (Courtesy of Tom Roberts.)

Andrew Henderson Alexander was born in North Carolina in 1829. He served in Company K, 56th North Carolina Infantry. He was a prisoner at Blackwell's Island, New York. A widower, Alexander married Eugenia McLean in February 1866. The following August, they moved to Florida. He was sheriff of Volusia County from 1868 to 1870 and served in the state legislature. In 1872, he built a home at Lake Beresford. (Courtesy of Tom Roberts.)

DeBary Hall was the winter retreat of German-born wine merchant Samuel Frederick DeBary. DeBary, who lived in New York, purchased land around Lake Monroe in 1870 to build his vacation home, which was completed in 1871. Guests at his estate included generals Ulysses Grant and William Tecumseh Sherman. DeBary Hall was listed in the National Register of Historic Places in 1972. (Courtesy of the West Volusia Historical Society.)

This guidon was proudly flown by the St. Johns Rangers, a cavalry militia company commanded by Capt. Benjamin Hopkins and Lt. Winston Stephens. The red and white fork-tail flag was made of silk and bore 13 stars in a triangular pattern. It was probably presented to the unit by women related to the soldiers. Sons of Confederate Veterans Camp No. 1360 in DeLand is named for the St. Johns Rangers. (Courtesy of Florida Department of State.)

Job Hart (left) was born in 1829 in Virginia. In 1862, he enlisted in Augusta Rifles, a Shenandoah militia, which became the 5th Virginia Infantry, Stonewall's Brigade. He was soon discharged under the conscription act as being overage. Then, in January 1863, he enlisted in Samuel B. Brown's Company, Richardson's Battalion, 13th Virginia Cavalry, which became the 39th Virginia Cavalry Battalion, Gen. Robert E. Lee's personal escort battalion. Hart's great-grandson Ron Alcorn (below, far left) is a member of John W. Morton's Battery, Forrest Cavalry Corps, which provides "the bang and the boom" for living histories, parades, Confederate memorial services and funerals, Southern Cross of Honor dedications, and reenactments. Pictured below are, from left to right, Ron Alcorn, Matt Alcorn, Joey Tann, Wilbur Dixon, Domonic Tuccio, Doug Brown (holding flag), unidentified, and Gene Hendrickson. (Both, courtesy of Ron Alcorn.)

Seven

Marion County is Dixie's Land

Marion County was established on March 14, 1844, from sections of Alachua, Hillsborough, and Mosquito Counties. It was named for Revolutionary War hero Gen. Francis Marion. Pictured here is the 1908 dedication of the Confederate monument at the Marion County courthouse in Ocala. The dedication was hosted by the J.J. Dickison Chapter No. 58, United Daughters of the Confederacy. The monument is now located in Ocala's Veterans' Park. (Courtesy of State Archives of Florida.)

Capt. John Jackson Dickison was born in Virginia and raised in South Carolina. In 1862, he organized Company H, 2nd Florida Cavalry. Dickison's successful exploits against Union forces made him a hero in Florida and earned him several nicknames, including the "Swamp Fox" and "Knight of the Silver Spurs." In *Confederate Military History* (1899), Dickison writes, "The grandest vindication of the South will come when Truth, no longer crushed to earth through narrow-mindedness and sectional prejudice, will write in golden characters a just tribute to every American soldier who fell on either side. Let the record be: 'Here lies an American Hero, a Martyr to the Right as his Conscience conceived it.' " The artist rendering below depicts J.J. Dickison (right) with Lt. Melton Haynes. (Left, courtesy of State Archives of Florida; below, artwork by and courtesy of Bob Grenier Sr.)

Mary Elizabeth Ling Dickison was born in Charleston, South Carolina, in 1820. She married Virginia-born cotton merchant John Jackson Dickison in 1845. With their four children, Charles, R.L., John, and Mary Elizabeth, they moved to Orange Lake, a settlement near Ocala, in 1856. They purchased a plantation they called Sunnyside. In 1890, Mary wrote the book *Dickison and His Men: Reminiscences of the War in Florida*. (Courtesy of State Archives of Florida.)

Jack Koblas was the author of 70 books and over 500 short stories, articles, screenplays, and poetry. He was the leading authority on the James-Younger Gang. His works include *J.J. Dickison: Swamp Fox of the Confederacy* and *The Swamp Fox and the Columbine*. Koblas was a member of the doo-wop band The Magpies, inducted into the Minnesota Rock & Country Hall of Fame. Koblas died in 2013. (Author's collection.)

This drawing depicts Capt. J.J. Dickison holding his son, Sgt. Charlie Dickison, who was shot through the heart near Palatka on August 2, 1864. As Charlie fell from his horse, he called out to Sgt. J.C. Crews, "Joe, I am killed!" Crews leapt from his horse, took Charlie in his arms, and called out for Capt. Dickison. When Dickison got to his son, he was dead. (Courtesy of State Archives of Florida.)

Charles Green Pearson was born in Newnansville, Alachua County, in 1843. He was sergeant major of the 6th Florida Infantry Battalion, which participated in the Battle of Olustee in February 1864. In May of that year, the battalion was sent to Richmond as part of Finegan's Brigade. Pearson was wounded at Totopotomoy Creek, north of Richmond. He died in 1870 and is buried in Orange Springs Community Church Cemetery. (Courtesy of Fred Donaldson.)

In 1864, Albertus Vogt (right) volunteered for the Confederate army at the age of 14. He was wounded twice, after which he was assigned as a guard at Andersonville Prison. Though Dr. C.A. Simmons is credited with the discovery of phosphate in Florida in 1883 near Gainesville, the Florida phosphate boom began after the 1889 discovery by Vogt near Dunnellon. Vogt noticed fossils of prehistoric animals in a spring on his property that reminded him of similar finds near phosphate deposits in South Carolina. His rock samples were determined to have very high phosphate content, so Vogt began buying up land in the area. The first hard rock production began in 1889 by the Marion Phosphate Company, followed by the Dunnellon Phosphate Company (below), in which Vogt had ownership interest. (Both, courtesy of the Greater Dunnellon Historical Society.)

John M. Martin was born in 1832 in South Carolina and was educated at The Citadel. In 1855, he moved to Marion County. Martin joined and was elected captain of the Marion Light Artillery in 1861. After being wounded, he served in the Confederate congress. He declined reelection and returned to the army as a colonel in the 9th Florida Infantry. (Courtesy of State Archives of Florida.)

Robert Fenwick Taylor was born in 1849 in South Carolina. When he was two, his family moved to Marion County. Taylor was a Confederate volunteer at the Battle of Gainesville. He married Amelia Haile in 1872, and they had two children. Taylor was appointed to the Florida Supreme Court in 1891 by Gov. Francis Fleming and served until 1925. Taylor died in 1928 in Tallahassee. (Courtesy of State Archives of Florida.)

In the 1880s, Union general Joshua Lawrence Chamberlain of Brunswick, Maine, became involved in a land development company called the Florida West Coast Improvement Company. The company had offices in seven cities, with its headquarters in Ocala. It constructed and operated the Silver Springs, Ocala & Gulf Railroad. Chamberlain sometimes acted as master and pilot of a steamboat that ran from Cedar Key to Homosassa. (Artwork by and courtesy of Bob Grenier Sr.)

Jehu Foster Marshall was born in 1817 in South Carolina. This portrait features Marshall as captain of the Abbeville Volunteers, Palmetto Regiment, during the Mexican War. After the war, he married Elizabeth DeBruhl, served in the South Carolina legislature, and operated a sugar plantation in Ocala. In 1862, he became the colonel of the 1st Regiment, South Carolina Rifles. He fell at Second Manassas. (Painting by William James Hubard.)

John J. Brown was born in 1847 in Columbia County, Florida. He enlisted in the Confederate army in 1861, but was discharged a year later for illness. In 1864 Brown reenlisted, joined his old outfit in Virginia, and became a corporal. He was captured and then imprisoned at Point Lookout, Maryland. Brown taught school in Marion County and was elected a Citrus County commissioner in 1887. (Courtesy of Byron Peavy.)

Harry Hurst (pictured) was born in 1940. He says, "I was blessed to start my life on a remote farm in Christmas, reared by a loving grandmother, Ozelma McDougle Canada. I am a proud fifth generation Floridan—not Floridian." In 1980, Hurst married Karen Gishbaugher of Pennsylvania. His Confederate ancestors include Andrew Allen and Enoch Hurst. Hurst is an officer in the Florida Division SCV. (Courtesy of Harry Hurst.)

Eight

Alachua, Micanopy, and Paynes Prairie

Alachua County was established in 1824. Its name possibly derives from the Timucuan word meaning "sink," which is how they described the region. Micanopy, named for a Seminole chief, was founded in 1821 and is one of Florida's earliest inland settlements. Micanopy is located on the south end of historic Paynes Prairie. In this 1925 photograph, Confederate veterans pose at the old Alachua County courthouse in Gainesville. (Courtesy of State Archives of Florida.)

Capt. Benjamin William Powell from Micanopy was born in 1826 and is an 1859 graduate of The Citadel. Immediately following Florida's secession on January 10, 1861, Powell organized three companies of local men to serve in the Confederate army. After the war, he returned to Micanopy and built a house of heart pine; today, it is a historic landmark. Powell died in 1901. (Courtesy of the Micanopy Historical Society Archives.)

James Mintor Croxton, pictured here in 1894, was born in 1847 in Montgomery County, Alabama. In August 1864, he was commissioned a second lieutenant by Gov. John Milton. Croxton served in Capt. William B. Watson's Company, known as the Orange Creek Company. The Orange Creek volunteers were attached to Munnerlyn's Special Cavalry Battalion. Croxton and his wife, Mary Beulah Pardee, lived in Micanopy. (Courtesy of the Micanopy Historical Society Archives.)

Josiah Thomas Walls was born a slave in Winchester, Virginia, in 1842. During the war, he fought in the 3rd Infantry Regiment, US Colored Troops, and later was transferred to the 35th Regiment, which was sent to Florida. After the war, he settled in Newnansville and married Helen Ferguson. Walls served in the Florida legislature, US Congress, as mayor of Gainesville, and as an Alachua County commissioner. (Courtesy of the Library of Congress.)

This plaque marks the site of Maj. James Bailey's cotton plantation. In 1853, Bailey sold 60 acres of his 2,000-acre plantation, to be used for the new city of Gainesville. During the war, Bailey sent supplies to Confederate troops. He died in March 1864 from meningitis contracted while building fortifications in Baldwin. His sons, Cosmo and Charles, enlisted in the Alachua Rebels, 7th Florida Infantry. (Courtesy of Carolyn Warner McGraw.)

Shown here in 1905 are, from left to right, (first row) William Daniel Holder, son Delton, and wife Josephine Wilkinson; (second row) daughter Edna, son Preston, and daughter Frieda. Holder served in Lutterloh's Company, Munnerlyn's Special Cavalry Battalion. He resided in Alachua and Levy Counties and is buried in the Jennings Lake Cemetery in Bell, which is near Trenton, the Gilchrist county seat. (Courtesy of Ann Williams and Tom Wilcox.)

The family of John Jacob Barr is seen here in 1905. They are, from left to right, (first row) grandchildren Clarice and John Watkins; (second row) son-in-law Dr. John Dixie Watkins, John Jacob Barr, his wife Sue Bauknight, and daughter Lillian Barr. John Jacob Barr served in the war while a cadet at The Citadel. He was a prominent Alachua County grower, known as the "Orange King." (Courtesy of the Micanopy Historical Society Archives.)

In 1854, Thomas Evans Haile and his wife, Esther Serena Chestnut, moved their family from South Carolina to Gainesville. They established a 1,500-acre Sea Island cotton plantation they named Kanapaha. Haile built a 6,200-square-foot home in 1856 that is one of the few remaining antebellum homes in Florida today. Haile served as first lieutenant in Capt. Melton Haynes's Company H, 5th Battalion, Florida Cavalry. (Courtesy of States Archives of Florida.)

Sgt. Edward Cooper Chitty was born in 1845 in South Carolina. He served in Company H, 17th South Carolina Infantry and was a prisoner at Point Lookout, Maryland. He and his wife, Mary Ann Cooper, moved to Micanopy in the 1890s, where they built this home in 1900. Shown here from left to right are Mary Ann Chitty (on the porch), Belle Chitty, and Charles Carter. (Courtesy of the Micanopy Historical Society Archives.)

Col. John Boston Dell was born in 1838 in Newnansville. In May 1862, he enlisted at Gainesville in Company F, 2nd Florida Cavalry. After the war, Dell engaged in farming near Trenton and was one of the largest planters in North Florida. He and his wife, Fannie Lassiter, moved their family to Gainesville in the 1880s. He served three terms in the Florida legislature. (Courtesy of Alachua County Library District.)

Rev. John Henry Tomkies, born in 1839 in Virginia, was the founder of Gainesville's First Baptist Church. Before the war, he moved to Madison, where he preached and taught school. Tomkies was a chaplain in the 7th Florida Infantry. After the war, he settled in Gainesville. He and his wife, Fannie Emma McCuen, raised three daughters and a son. (Courtesy of Alachua County Library District.)

Theodore H. Willard, pictured here with Dude, an orphaned boy he raised, was the captain of Company C, Florida Reserves CSA. Willard served as sheriff of Madison County from 1877 to 1880, state senator from Madison in 1881, state representative from Alachua County in 1903, and mayor of High Springs from 1910 to 1911. He married Alice Roberta Brown in High Springs on July 9, 1898. (Courtesy of State Archives of Florida.)

John E. Gavin was born in 1823 in North Carolina. He married Mahala Grantham in Georgia on November 14, 1848. The couple moved to Alachua County in 1858. Gavin served in Company A, 9th Florida Infantry. The Gavin family owned a farm at Fort McCoy in Marion County, eventually moving to Hillsborough County. They then settled in Polk County around 1880. (Courtesy of L. Rabun Battle.)

Madison Starke Perry came to Florida in 1845 from Lancaster County, South Carolina, and helped establish the village of Rochelle. He was elected Florida's fourth governor in 1856. On January 10, 1861, while Perry was in office, Florida seceded from the Union. After his term ended, he became colonel of the 7th Florida Infantry until illness forced his resignation in April 1863. Perry died at his plantation in March 1865. The Rochelle School was established on land donated by his daughter, Sallie Perry, in 1885, and was called the Martha Perry Institute, named for Perry's wife. Perry is buried at Oak Ridge Cemetery on land he set aside in 1854 for the community. His son, Madison Starke Perry Jr., was also a Confederate veteran, who served in Company C, 2nd Florida Cavalry. Neither of Perry's children married. (Both, author's collection.)

Nine

PUTNAM, CONFEDERATE SPY SISTERS, AND MARGARET'S HIBERNIA

Putnam County, established in 1849, was named for soldier, statesman, judge, and first president of the Florida Historical Society, Benjamin Alexander Putnam. North of Palatka on the St. Johns River was Hibernia, the plantation home of Col. Lewis Fleming and his wife, Margaret, memorialized in the novel *Margaret's Story* by Eugenia Price. Pictured here are Union and Confederate veterans in Palatka. (Courtesy of Putnam County Headquarters Library.)

Winston J.T. Stephens was born in 1829 in Georgia. He married Octavia "Tivie" Bryant in November 1859, and the couple settled at Rose Cottage in Welaka. Stephens enlisted in 1861 as first lieutenant of the St. Johns Rangers, and was promoted to captain in 1862. Stephens survived the Battle of Olustee in February 1864, only to die a fortnight later from a sniper bullet while on patrol. (Courtesy of State Archives of Florida.)

Harry A. Gray (standing on porch left of door) and his wife, Eliza Wadell, sitting to his right, are pictured at their home in Palatka. Gray was the captain of Company B, 2nd Florida Cavalry, attached to Capt. J.J. Dickison's command. In November 1880, Gray sold his steamboat *Marion* to Col. Hubbard L. Hart, owner of the Hart Line, but stayed on as the *Marion's* skipper. (Courtesy of Putnam County Headquarters Library.)

Maria Dolores "Lola" Sánchez (right), along with her sisters, Francesca "Panchita" (below) and Eugenia, were spies for the Confederate army. Lola became upset when their father was falsely accused of being a spy by the Union army and imprisoned. On May 21, 1864, Union officers arrived at the Sánchez residence and were served supper. During the meal, the officers felt confident to discuss their plans for a raid the next morning against the Confederates. Lola overheard the conversation and told her sisters. Panchita entertained the officers while Eugenia prepared supper. Lola left the house and crossed the St. Johns River to meet with Capt. J.J. Dickison. She told him of the plan and returned home. Her action resulted in Dickison's surprise ambush and the sinking of the USS *Columbine*. (Right, artwork by Andrea Seitz Binkley; below, courtesy of Susan Buckley.)

This plaque marks the site where, on May 23, 1864, Capt. J.J. Dickison captured the Union gunboat USS *Columbine*. Hoping to trap the Confederates on the east side of the St. Johns River, the *Columbine* was sent upriver. Dickison, however, had already crossed the river and set the ambush at Horse Landing. It is the only known incident in history in which a cavalry unit sank an enemy gunboat. (Author's collection.)

The Confederate Memorial at the Putnam County courthouse in Palatka was erected in 1924 by the Patton Anderson Chapter of the United Daughters of the Confederacy. The monument consists of a bronze statue of a Confederate soldier atop a solid granite base. Located along the sidewalk encircling the monument are four types of artillery projectiles. (Courtesy of Putnam County Headquarters Library.)

Hubbard L. Hart's steamboat line began transporting people and supplies in 1860. During the war, Hart ferried goods for the Confederacy to blockade runners along the St. Johns River. Hart invented the inboard paddleboat in 1866, launching the *Griffin*. This new design was featured in the 1893 Chicago World's Fair. Pictured here are guests aboard Hart's newly acquired steamboat, the *Osceola*. In 1895, Hart was killed in a fall from a streetcar in Atlanta. (Courtesy of Putnam County Headquarters Library.)

Dr. George Elias Hawes was born in 1816 in South Carolina. He moved to Palatka in 1854. Hawes, one of Palatka's earliest doctors, served in the Florida legislature and fought in the 2nd Florida Infantry. He created the silver spurs that were presented to Capt. J.J. Dickison as a gift from the ladies of Orange Springs, fashioning them from trinkets the ladies donated. (Courtesy of Putnam County Headquarters Library.)

Capt. Francis Philip Fleming (left) was born in 1841 in Duval County, the son of Lewis and Margaret Seton Fleming of Hibernia. He commanded a volunteer company at the Battle of Natural Bridge near the St. Marks River on March 6, 1865. He studied law and was admitted to the bar in 1868. In 1871, he married Floride Lydia Pearson (below), the daughter of Florida Supreme Court justice Bird Pearson. Fleming served as Florida's governor from 1889 to 1893. After his term as governor, he served on the board of trustees of the new Florida Old Confederate Soldiers and Sailors Home. Floride was a charter member of the Martha Reid Chapter No. 19, United Daughters of the Confederacy, the oldest chapter in the state of Florida. In 1921, she was the honorary president of the Florida Division UDC. (Both, courtesy of State Archives of Florida.)

The above photograph shows the Fleming family at Hibernia in the 1890s. Margaret Seton "Maggie" Fleming is seated at center in a white blouse. The Flemings were noted planters, military officers, lawyers, hoteliers, and politicians. During the war, Maggie's mother, Margaret, and Maggie's daughters were left alone at Hibernia while the Fleming sons served in the Confederate army. Margaret was falsely accused of being a spy and was expelled from Hibernia by Union troops. She and her daughters spent the war nursing the wounded and sick at a Confederate hospital at Lake City. After the war, the Flemings returned to Hibernia. Their home was still standing, but it had been stripped of all furnishings. The family restored and refurnished the house and opened it as a hotel. Below, Gov. Francis Fleming (seated at far right) visits a Florida National Guard encampment around 1890. (Both, courtesy of State Archives of Florida.)

Lt. Col. Albert H. Wilcoxson (left) commanded the 17th Connecticut Infantry at the Battle of Braddock's Farm on February 5, 1865. Wilcoxson, who had been raiding farms for supplies, was returning to his headquarters with 10 wagons of cotton when he was surprised by Capt. J.J. Dickison. Wilcoxson mounted his horse and charged. After he fired his last shot from his pistol, he drew his sword and again charged Dickison, who shot him. When the fight ended, Dickison asked the mortally wounded Wilcoxson, "Colonel, why did you throw your life away?" To which Wilcoxson replied, "Don't blame yourself; you are only doing your duty as a soldier. I alone am to blame." Wilcoxson died later in Tallahassee. Upon request from Wilcoxson's wife, Martha, Dickison returned the officer's sword to her. (Left, artwork by and courtesy of Bob Grenier Sr.; below, State Archives of Florida.)

Ten

Florida's Gallant Sons

After Florida seceded from the Union on January 10, 1861, several unofficial state flags flew until the legislature completed work on February 1 on an act to establish an official state flag. Gov. Madison Perry designed a flag (pictured), modeled after the first national flag of the Confederacy, known as the Stars and Bars. He added the newly created seal of Florida to a blue field. (Courtesy of State Archives of Florida.)

Gen. Truman Seymour commanded the Union troops at the Battle of Olustee, also known as Ocean Pond. It was the largest battle fought in Florida. On February 20, 1864, Seymour's force of 5,500 men met a Confederate force of about 5,000 commanded by Gen. Joseph Finegan. The battle, a Confederate victory, produced some of the heaviest losses, by percentage, of any major battle of the war. (Courtesy of State Archives of Florida.)

John Whittier Messer Appleton was the captain of Company A, 54th Massachusetts Infantry during the attack on Fort Wagner, South Carolina, on July 18, 1863. He rose to major of the 54th Massachusetts, which was one of the first official "colored" units of the war. During the Battle of Olustee, Appleton stayed at Barber's Plantation to protect the Union's rear guard. (Courtesy of State Archives of Florida.)

Giles Mosely Pease was born in 1839 in Boston. He mustered into the Union army as a second lieutenant on August 3, 1863. Pease served as an assistant surgeon with the 54th Massachusetts Infantry Regiment. After the Battle of Olustee, while the regiment was in Jacksonville, there were a number of changes in assignments and posts. On May 28, 1864, Pease resigned for reasons of disability. (Courtesy of State Archives of Florida.)

At Olustee, the 54th Massachusetts Infantry was the last regiment fighting the Confederates, falling back when their ammunition ran out. Of the regiment's 500 men, 86 were killed or wounded. The story of the 54th Massachusetts was told in the film *Glory*. Shown here are, from left to right, (top row) Jeremiah Rolls and Abram Simms; (middle row) George Lipscomb and Thomas Bowman; (bottom row) Isom Ampey and John Wilson. (Courtesy of State Archives of Florida.)

Col. George Paul Harrison Jr. was 22 years old when he commanded the 2nd Confederate Infantry Brigade at Olustee, which included the 1st Florida Battalion, 1st Georgia Regulars, 32nd Georgia Infantry, 64th Georgia Infantry, Guerard's Battery, and the 28th Georgia Heavy Artillery Battalion, also known as "Bonaud's Battalion." After the war, Harrison was a lawyer in Alabama. He was married four times. (Courtesy of State Archives of Florida.)

Joseph Roswell Hawley assisted Col. Alfred H. Terry in raising the 7th Connecticut Infantry in 1861 and was named lieutenant colonel. Hawley was in John Milton Brannan's expedition to Florida in January 1863, and he commanded the post at Fernandina. He commanded a brigade under Gen. Truman Seymour at Olustee. Hawley served as the 25th governor of Connecticut and served in the US House of Representatives and Senate. (Courtesy of State Archives of Florida.)

Loomis L. Langdon was a Union artillery officer. In February 1861, he was sent to Fort Pickens from Fort Monroe, Virginia, on the frigate USS *Brooklyn*. Also that year, he defended against an attack by the Confederates at the US Navy Yard and at Fort Barrancas, located on the western tip of Santa Rosa Island. Langdon commanded a battalion of field batteries at the Battle of Olustee. (Courtesy of State Archives of Florida.)

Wilkinson Call, a lawyer in Jacksonville, was the assistant adjutant general on Gen. Joseph Finegan's staff at the Battle of Olustee. In 1865, Call was elected to the US Senate. During the confusion of early Reconstruction policies, he was denied admission, and Florida remained unrepresented until 1868. When Call was reelected in 1879, a more amenable Senate, willing to forget his Confederate service, seated Call. (Courtesy of State Archives of Florida.)

Sgt. James Barnard Cone (left) and Capt. William Haddock Cone were the second and fourth sons of Capt. William Henry Cone II and Sarah Haddock Cone. James and William, along with their brothers, Lt. Simon Peter and Capt. Charles Floyd, served in the 2nd Florida Cavalry and fought in the Battle of Olustee. William Haddock was the father of Florida governor Frederick Preston Cone. (Courtesy of State Archives of Florida.)

The Tompkins brothers are pictured here in the late 1890s. They are, from left to right, (first row) David L. and Joseph Robert; (second row) James Andrew and Wilson Peek. They were the sons of John and Ann Pearce Tompkins of Alachua County. The brothers served in the 2nd Florida Cavalry and survived the Battle of Olustee. (Courtesy of State Archives of Florida.)

On March 5, 1951, Mrs. M.C. Moore unveiled a monument at the Olustee Battlefield dedicated to Gen. Joseph Finegan, the victorious general at the battle. The monument was a gift from the United Daughters of the Confederacy. Moore was the president of the Martha Reid Chapter No. 19 in Jacksonville. Rep. Robert Burnsed of Baker County received the marker on behalf of the park. (Courtesy of State Archives of Florida.)

In 1897, the Florida Division of the United Daughters of the Confederacy began raising funds to place a monument at the Olustee Battlefield. The Florida legislature appropriated $2,500 and established a commission to oversee the construction. The monument was completed in 1912 and dedicated on October 23 of that year. Today, the Olustee Battlefield Historic State Park is administered by the Florida Department of Environmental Protection. (Courtesy of State Archives of Florida.)

Bunberry Haynes was born in 1832 in North Carolina. He came to Florida in 1845 with his brother, Confederate cavalry captain Melton Haynes. Bunberry Haynes enlisted in Gainesville and served in Company C, 2nd Florida Cavalry. He then transferred to Company H. He was a postmaster and justice of the peace in Alachua County. After the war, he was a tax collector for Bradford County. (Courtesy of the Haynes Family Collection.)

Confederate captain Richard H. Bradford enlisted in March 1861. He was the first Florida officer to die in the war, when, on the morning of October 9, 1861, he was instantly killed while leading his men at the battle of Santa Rosa Island. Gov. John Milton delivered the eulogy at Bradford's funeral. New River County was renamed Bradford County on December 6, 1861, in his honor. (Courtesy of State Archives of Florida.)

Theodore Washington Brevard (second row, right) moved to Florida in 1847. He married Mary Laura Call, a daughter of Gov. Richard Call, in 1859. Brevard served as state comptroller and in the Florida legislature. He commanded a battalion of rangers at Olustee and served in Virginia with the 11th Florida Infantry, where he was elevated to the rank of colonel. Brevard County was named for him. (Courtesy of State Archives of Florida.)

Henry Theodore Titus operated a sawmill in Jacksonville until he moved to Kansas in 1856 to join pro-slavery forces. Titus returned to Jacksonville during the war and served as a quartermaster in the Florida Militia. In 1867, he settled at Sand Point, where he opened a general store and hotel. In 1873, while serving as the postmaster, he changed the name of the town to Titusville. (Courtesy of State Archives of Florida.)

Joseph Wellington Rosier, pictured here in the early 1900s, was born in 1863 in Dothan, Alabama. He was the son of Efrin and Eliza Rosier, who were slaves on a large cotton plantation. He and his wife, Julia, lived in Jacksonville and had 13 children, born between 1885 and 1913. (Courtesy of State Archives of Florida.)

On May 6–9, 1914, over 70,000 visitors, including 8,000 Confederate veterans, converged in Jacksonville for the 24th annual national reunion of the United Confederate Veterans. The city expected no more than 25,000 people. Gov. Park Trammell welcomed the visiting veterans. Capt. John Livingston Inglis, riding the horse at far right, served in Company D, 3rd Florida Infantry. The average age of the veterans was 74 years old. (Courtesy of State Archives of Florida.)

John E. Spoon, pictured at his home in Pensacola in the 1930s, was the last living Confederate veteran in Escambia County. He served as a private in Company I, 17th Alabama Infantry, and as a corporal in Company C, 2nd Regiment, Corps of Army Engineers. The inscription on the badge Spoon is wearing reads "Camp Ward No. 10 UCV Pensacola." Note that the flag is upside-down. (Courtesy of State Archives of Florida.)

Railroad magnate Henry Morrison Flagler was born in 1830 in New York. In 1862, Flagler and his brother-in-law, Barney York, founded the Flagler & York Salt Company, a salt mining business in Saginaw, Michigan. When the war ended, however, salt, which had been in heavy use as a preservative by the Union army, was no longer in high demand, and the Flagler & York Salt Company collapsed. (Courtesy of State Archives of Florida.)

Mary McLeod was the maid of honor for the Florida Division of the National Convention of the United Confederate Veterans at the annual reunion in Birmingham, Alabama. The 36th annual reunion was held on May 18–22, 1926. "The Magic City" hosted the 1894, 1908, 1916, and 1926 UCV reunions. (Courtesy of State Archives of Florida.)

Members of the Florida Monument Commission are, from left to right, Col. Walter Moore, Col. David Lang, Capt. William Duncan Ballantine, Maj. William M. Robbins, and Col. John P. Nicholson. The commission was visiting Devil's Den at Gettysburg on July 6, 1895, to pick out a site for a Florida monument. It was not until July 3, 1963, that Florida erected and dedicated a monument at Gettysburg. (Courtesy of State Archives of Florida.)

William W. Wilson was a lieutenant in Company G, 8th Florida Infantry, when he was wounded in the arm and captured at Gettysburg on July 3, 1863. He was a prisoner at Johnson's Island, Ohio, and then released at Fort Delaware. After the war, Wilson opened an insurance company. In 1907, Wilson's wife, M. Nicholson, filed for a widow's pension claim in Gadsden County. (Courtesy of State Archives of Florida.)

Richard B. Waller was born on July 5, 1842, in Nolensville, Tennessee. He enlisted in the Confederate army on July 9, 1861, and served in Capt. Theodore Brevard's Company D, 2nd Florida Infantry, known as the "Leon Rifles." In December 1886, Waller homesteaded in Hernando County. He was married three times. He died on September 10, 1930, in New Hope, Washington County. (Courtesy of State Archives of Florida.)

Charles James Munnerlyn (left) was elected as a representative to the Confederate congress from 1862 to 1864. He then received a major's commission from Pres. Jefferson Davis, who ordered him to Florida to organize a regiment. His duty was to provide a steady flow of supplies, especially cattle, to the starving army in Virginia. The regiment Munnerlyn commanded was combined with other regiments to become the 1st Battalion Florida Special Cavalry, which he commanded as a lieutenant colonel. This cavalry battalion was often referred to as the Cattle Battalion, Cow Cavalry, Commissary Battalion, or Munnerlyn's Battalion. It was composed of nearly 800 soldiers. The Cow Cavalry Monument in Plant City (below) was erected in 2007 by the Plant City Chapter No. 1931, UDC. (Left, courtesy of State Archives of Florida; below, courtesy of Carolyn Warner McGraw.)

Pictured here are, from left to right, an unidentified Confederate veteran kissing the flag; Ohioans William Alcorn, Emery Potter, and Eli Bourdo; and John Reardon, commander of the Sons of Confederate Veterans. The men from Ohio returned a Confederate battle flag they had captured during the war. This photograph was taken at the United Confederate Veterans reunion in Marianna on September 26–29, 1927. (Courtesy of State Archives of Florida.)

John Stephen Sargent (left), pictured wearing his GAR sash, was born in 1846 in Hutton, Illinois. He served in Company C, 68th Illinois Infantry. In 1892, Sargent joined Koreshan Unity, a communal utopia formed by Cyrus Teed, who took the name "Koresh" (Persian for his name, Cyrus). Teed took his followers to Estero, Florida, to form his "New Jerusalem" in 1894. (Courtesy of State Archives of Florida.)

Gen. David Lang served as a sergeant in Company H, 1st Florida Infantry, and later as captain of Company C, 8th Florida Infantry. He was wounded at the battles of Antietam and Fredericksburg. Lang was promoted to colonel of the 8th Florida in 1863 and fought at Chancellorsville. On July 2, 1863, he led Perry's Brigade against the Union's defensive line on Cemetery Ridge at Gettysburg. (Courtesy of State Archives of Florida.)

Pictured in this April 1905 photograph are, from left to right, state printer Thomas Jefferson Appleyard, Gov. Napoleon Bonaparte Broward, former governor Francis Fleming, and Fred Robertson. The photograph was taken at the capitol in Tallahassee. The governor accepted Confederate battle flags captured from Florida during the war and ordered returned by the War Department in Washington. (Courtesy of State Archives of Florida.)

John B. Fletcher served in Company L, 1st Regiment Florida Infantry Reserves. He was a veteran of the 1865 Battle of Natural Bridge. Fletcher erected monuments along the road on the western side of the bridge. The first monument was brick and cement, with a cannonball on top, and set in slabs of marble honoring individuals and units. It was unveiled on July 4, 1919. (Courtesy of State Archives of Florida.)

This 1861 photograph features the women of the Ladies Soldiers Friend Sewing Society in Tallahassee. The society existed during the entire War Between the States. Shortly after the war, the group renamed itself the Tallahassee Memorial Association. Then, in 1898, the association organized itself as the Anna Jackson Chapter No. 224, UDC, which is still active today. (Courtesy of State Archives of Florida.)

Lawrence "Laurie" M. Anderson of Tallahassee was a member of Company A, Bradford Light Infantry, Florida Battalion. He died on April 7, 1862, the second day of fighting at the Battle of Shiloh in Tennessee. Shiloh, also known as the Battle of Pittsburg Landing, was a significant battle in the "western theater" of the war. It was a Union victory. (Courtesy of State Archives of Florida.)

The Confederate flag flew over Florida's capitol dome on March 6, 1963, to mark the 98th anniversary of the Battle of Natural Bridge, in which Union troops were halted in an advance on Tallahassee. The flag was hoisted by Horace Marsh of Jacksonville and Tommy King of Pensacola, members of Kappa Alpha fraternity at Florida State University. The fraternity traditionally honors the anniversary of the battle. (Courtesy of State Archives of Florida.)

Secretary of State Tom Adams holds a Confederate battle flag with UDC historian Mrs. E.A. Hayden on October 5, 1961, in Tallahassee. The flag was discovered hidden in the eave of an antebellum house that had been torn down in 1930. The flag was thought to have been flown at the Battle of Natural Bridge. (Courtesy of State Archives of Florida.)

Author Susan Bradford Eppes was born in 1846 in Bradfordville. She was the granddaughter of John Branch, the last territorial governor of Florida. In 1866, she married Lt. Nicholas Eppes, whom she referred to as "My Soldier in Gray" in her 1925 book *Through Some Eventful Years*. Lieutenant Eppes served in Company H, 1st Florida Cavalry. In 1920, Susan was the honorary president of the Florida Division UDC. (Courtesy of State Archives of Florida.)

This 1920s photograph features Confederate veterans at the Maj. Robert Gamble Plantation in Ellenton. During the war, the mansion was occupied by Capt. Archibald McNeill, a Confederate blockade runner. In 1925, the mansion and grounds were bought by the UDC and donated to the state as a memorial to Judah P. Benjamin. In 1937, the UDC installed a memorial plaque to Benjamin at the mansion. (Courtesy of State Archives of Florida.)

Florida Division SCV commander John Reardon (second from left) joins Confederate veterans and their families at the United Confederate Veterans reunion in Marianna on September 26–29, 1927. The UCV, established in 1889, was a benevolent, historical, social, and literary association for Confederate veterans. The UCV was active into the 1940s; its final reunion was held in Norfolk, Virginia, in 1951. (Courtesy of State Archives of Florida.)

This plaque to Dr. Samuel Mudd was installed in March 1961 at Fort Jefferson in the Dry Tortugas. Mudd was imprisoned on July 24, 1865, for the Lincoln assassination conspiracy. When yellow fever broke out at the fort in 1867, he cared for the sick and saved many lives. Mudd earned admiration and gratitude for his service. Pres. Andrew Johnson pardoned Mudd on February 6, 1869. (Courtesy of State Archives of Florida.)

In January 1955, Florida's oldest Confederate veteran, "Uncle" Billy Lundy, celebrated his 107th birthday at Eglin Air Force Base in Valparaiso. Lundy was born on January 18, 1848, in Coffee Springs, Alabama. He was a member of Company D, 4th Alabama Cavalry Regiment. Lundy died on September 1, 1957, in Crestview, Florida, at the age of 109. (Courtesy of State Archives of Florida.)

William Felix Mickler was born in St. Augustine in 1836. He was a civil engineer who fought in the Seminole Indian Wars and served in the Florida House of Representatives. He was the last surviving member of Florida's secession convention. Mickler served in Capt. William Cone's company in Scott's Battalion. He helped plant torpedoes in the St. Johns River and fought at the Battle of Olustee. (Courtesy of State Archives of Florida.)

This 1891 photograph features the Confederate monument in St. Augustine draped for Robert E. Lee's death. This monument is a larger, rebuilt version of the original monument, which was denied a location on any government property by the military governor, Col. John Sprague. The Ladies Memorial Association persevered, and the monument was placed along St. George Street, in front of the home of Bishop Augustin Verot. (Courtesy of State Archives of Florida.)

Gen. Edmund Kirby Smith (seated) was born in 1824 in St. Augustine. He served as chief of staff to Gen. Joseph E. Johnston at Harper's Ferry and helped organize the Army of the Shenandoah. In January 1863, Smith was sent to command the Trans-Mississippi Department, which encompasses Texas, Louisiana, Arkansas, and the Indian Territory. In June 1865, Smith surrendered the last Confederate forces at Galveston, Texas. (Courtesy of State Archives of Florida.)

Cows were one of the most important participants in the war. Moving beef to where it was needed became a profitable, and very dangerous, occupation. Ranchers and cowboys formed battalions called the "Cow Cavalry" to defend against Union attacks as they moved the cows to holding pens in North Florida. Florida scrub cows, or "cracker" cows, are the descendants of the livestock brought over by Spanish explorers. (Courtesy of Florida State Parks.)

Doug David Dawson (center) was born in Pensacola in 1945. In 1969, he married Sherry Ann Davis. Dawson, a retired USN firefighter captain, joined the Stephen R. Mallory SCV camp in 1997. He became the Florida Division commander in 2004, and in that position, diligently worked for the "Confederate Cause." Dawson passed away on October 30, 2012. Pictured here with Dawson are Bob Grenier and Lainie deMaine Cross. (Author's collection.)

Karen and Harry Hurst pose at the Lee-Jackson Cotillion in St. Augustine in January 2006. Karen, a Pennsylvanian, is described by her Florida-native husband as a "Northern Lady with a true Southern Soul." She is a charter member and president of the Sarah Isabella Haynes Chapter No. 10, Order of Confederate Rose, which received its charter at the SCV reunion in Lake City in May 2006. (Author's collection.)

Pictured at the 2013 Florida Division Sons of Confederate Veterans reunion in Ocala are, from left to right, Judy Davis, Jim Davis, and Dale Cox. Florida Division Commander Jim Davis has led the SCV in a series of heritage victories and milestones during his tenure. Judy is a member of Ancient City No. 2232, UDC. Cox, from Two Egg, is a southern writer and historian. (Author's collection.)

Florida Division SCV 8th Brigade commander Charles "Chuck" B. Kadel (left) presents "Yankee Bob" Grenier a passport to travel the Confederate States of America at the 2013 Pvt. William Riley Milton Camp No. 741 Lee-Jackson Banquet in Fruitland Park. Kadel, a dedicated scholar of Southern heritage, is also the commander of Maj. Gen. John C. Breckinridge Camp No. 1786 in Oxford. (Author's collection.)

The Dixie Belles performing troupe is composed of Nancy Solomon (left), Becky Bathen (center), and Nansea Markham Miller. The Dixie Belles, pictured here in 2013 at the inaugural Rifles, Rails & History event in Tavares, is dedicated to honoring Confederate heritage through performing original dances and theatricals set to music popular during the War Between the States. Nansea is the director, choreographer, and author. (Author's collection.)

This half-scale replica of the Confederate submarine *H.L. Hunley* is based in Jacksonville. Built in 2010, it was donated to Kirby Smith Camp No. 1209, which puts plenty of miles on the replica as it visits schools and participates in many events. The story of the original *Hunley*'s role in the war, as well as its discovery, recovery, and preservation, is an extraordinary and fascinating chronicle of American history. (Author's collection.)

The Rifles, Rails & History Color Guard march down Main Street in Tavares. Shown here are, from left to right, Capt. Ken Baum, Corp. Don Campbell, Bob Grenier, Corp. Ken Plemons, and 1st Sgt. Mark Prive. A unique aspect of the Rifles, Rails & History event is that it was not held in a distant battlefield, but in the heart of downtown Tavares, a city committed to honoring its history. (Author's collection.)

Union and Confederate infantry, cavalry, artillery, and navy reenactors pause to salute and honor the Tavares "Freedom Flag" (not pictured) during the Rifles, Rails & History parade on Saturday morning, September 28, 2013. The spectacular and inspiring Freedom Flag, located at the Sinclair Avenue and Main Street roundabout, was dedicated on February 16, 2013. (Photograph by Brian Whicher, courtesy of Rifles, Rails & History.)

Al Stone, pictured with his wife, Shirley, in Tavares in 2013, portrayed Gen. Robert E. Lee in the History Channel's documentary *April 1865*. He has portrayed Lee at Stratford Hall, Lee's birthplace, for several years. In 2007, he was accepted by Robert E. Lee IV as offering the most accurate impression available. Stone has shared billing at events with artist Mort Kunstler and historian Dr. James Robertson. (Author's collection.)

Keith Kohl (left) and Steve Boettcher pose at the Confederate headquarters at Rifles, Rails & History. Kohl, who resides in Ocala, is a writer, lecturer, and the commander of the 2nd Florida Battalion in one of Florida's largest reenactor organizations. A premiere Florida historian, Kohl authored the book *Florida's Civil War Years*. Boettcher, who also portrays Abraham Lincoln, has helped organize the Ocklawaha River Raid for over 20 years. (Author's collection.)

Keith Kohl escorts Heather Dawn Kendrick Graham to the dance floor for the Virginia Reel at the Rifles, Rails & History cotillion. Graham is a business owner and the publisher of *Focus* magazine. As a civic leader, she works to attract visitors to Tavares's downtown historic and entertainment district. Her inaugural RR&H event was an extraordinary entertainment and educational experience, as well as a huge economic success. (Courtesy of Don Campbell.)

At the RR&H event, Byron Peavy (right) noticed a caregiver pushing a handicapped woman in a wheelchair. The woman had done horse therapy, so Peavy unhooked his horse, Diablo, from the tether line, and, for a moment, Diablo held his head inches from the woman's chest. The nurse was in tears, and Peavy fought back his. Peavy says, "Diablo is not just a horse, he is my best friend." (Author's collection.)

Annette Lindsey was born and raised in Gainesville. She is a member of Olustee Chapter No. 2488, UDC; director of the Black Hawk Cavalry Chapter No. 856, Children of the Confederacy; president of the Seahorse Key Lighthouse Chapter No. 25, Order of Confederate Rose; and works closely with the John Hance O'Steen Camp No. 770, SCV. Lindsey and her father, Clement Lindsey, prepare the pyrotechnics at reenactments. (Author's collection.)

Aimee Lee and Bryan Gilmore were married on March 11, 2000. Lee is a sixth-generation Floridian. Her great-great-grandfather, Samuel Augustus Miley, served in Company K, 4th Florida Infantry. She is a charter member of the Mary and Mollie Bell Chapter No. 20, OCR. Texas-born Gilmore is a member of the Jubal Early Camp No. 556, SCV and is a distant cousin of the camp's namesake. (Author's collection.)

This photograph, taken at the 2010 Tavares Independence Day "Where Dreams Take Flight" celebration, features the ladies from the Florida Society, Order of Confederate Rose. They are, from left to right in front, Catherine Peavy, Kathleen Carter, Annette Lindsey, Karen Hurst, and JoEllen Rowe. The group's parade entry, "Councilman Bob Grenier presents the Blue and the Gray in United We Stand," received the Best Overall Award for their participation. (Author's collection.)

Chicagoan Bob Grenier was a guest speaker at the Capt. Melton Haynes Southern Cross of Honor dedication at the Yalaha Cemetery on November 23, 2013. Grenier credits a 1999 vacation to Gettysburg with his mom and dad, the discovery and preservation of the historic Woodlea house, and his "crashing" of a Sons of Confederate Veterans meeting, with changing forever the course of his life. (Courtesy of Sanda Crabtree Mott.)

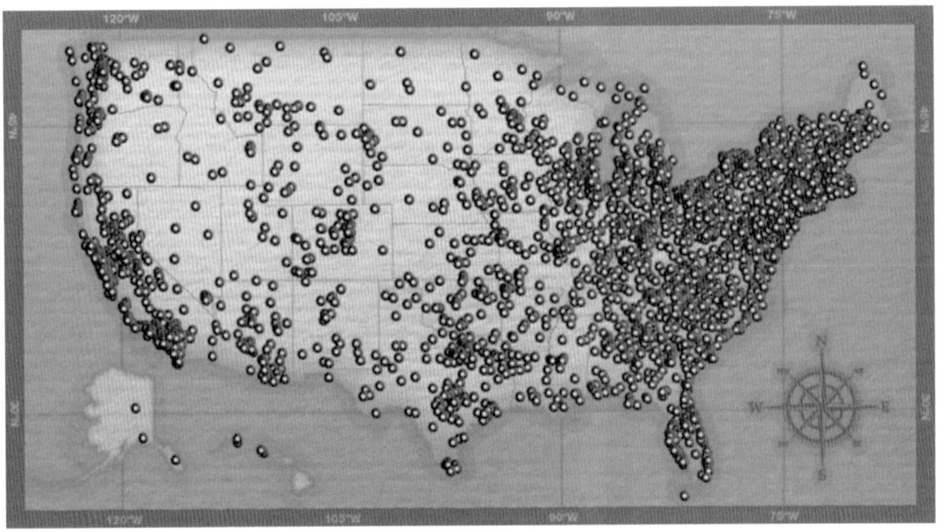